Widow's Walk

WANDERING IN THE WILDERNESS OF GRIEF

Barbara Fusco

ISBN 978-1-63575-331-8 (Paperback)
ISBN 978-1-63575-333-2 (Hard Cover)
ISBN 978-1-63575-332-5 (Digital)

Christian Faith Publishing, Inc.
296 Chestnut Street
Meadville, PA 16335
www.christianfaithpublishing.com

Printed in the United States of America

Contents

Don't You Have Family in New Jersey?

Monday morning, my husband Gene and I are on our way home to Chincoteague Island, Virginia, after spending Easter with family in New Jersey. We want to hurry up and get back, but we first have to make a stop. He hasn't felt right since Friday, and a local doctor had told him to get an X-ray after the weekend. So arm in arm, we enter Peninsula Regional Hospital, hoping to have this over quickly and be on our way.

We fill out the necessary paperwork, and Gene is taken in for X-rays. After what seems a very long time, a doctor comes out to me.

"Your husband has to be rushed to OR. He needs to have a chest tube put in to drain pleural fluid. He has a tumor. Every one we have seen like this is malignant. Don't you have family in New Jersey? We think you'd better go back there."

Shattered, I wait for Gene to get settled in his room. We spend the rest of the day in shock, trying to process this news, trying to encourage one another. As darkness falls, I tear myself away from him.

Alone, for the third time in our thirty-four-year marriage, I drive to Chincoteague in freezing rain and snow. A forty-mile-an-hour wind howls across the bay, mirroring the chaos in my soul.

I can't bear the thought of going home. Abandoned and alone, I stop to tell dear friends, Betty and Art, what has happened. What a godsend they are. Betty, then in her seventies—a three-time cancer survivor—is full of spirit, life, hope, and love. I'm starving for her company, but I can't delay going home forever.

All night sleep eludes me as wild wind shakes the old house and shock and fear shake me. I can't stop trembling. My entire adult life had been spent bound to this man, and the prospect of losing him is wrenching.

Ritual and Wandering

Ritual

Ritual, as defined by *Webster*, is a stereotyped sequence of activities performed in a sequestered place,—which involves gestures, words, and objects. The pump of inspiration is primed by ritual. When my husband was diagnosed with lung cancer, I began an early morning ritual, which became my sanity and my salvation. Upon waking, I would go downstairs to make coffee and return to my bed. There I would read scripture, pray, and write my feelings: the good, the bad, and the ugly. Essential objects were a Bible, spiral-bound notebook, Paper Mate SharpWriter, and coffee. The minute I returned to the bed, I was aware that I was in the presence of God. This ritual resulted in the writings upon which this work is based. My journal became my friend and counselor, a gateway to self-awareness.

Wandering

Wandering in the wilderness of grief is a perfect metaphor for my theological and psychological journey during early widowhood.

I have attempted to be transparent, honest, and hopeful.

Island

If once you have slept on an island,
You'll never be quite the same;
You may go by the same old name,
You look as you looked the day before
And may bustle about in street and shop
You may sit at home and sew,
But you'll see blue water and wheeling gulls
Wherever your feet may go.
You may chat with the neighbors of this and that
And close to your fire keep,
But you'll hear ship whistle and lighthouse bell
And tides beat through your sleep.
Oh, you won't know why and you can't say how
Such a change upon you came,
But once you've slept on an island, you'll never be quite the same.

Rachael Lyman Field (September 19, 1894–March 15, 1942)

Heart's Home

"If once you have slept on an island, you'll never be quite the same."

So begins Rachael Field's poem, and we have never been the same. I sit on the porch, thirty years after falling in love with this place, looking at the water, listening to the wheeling gulls and remembering the past.

Chincoteague Island, which has left me "never quite the same," is located in the far northeastern portion of Virginia's Eastern Shore—a peninsula bound on the west by the Chesapeake Bay, and the east by the Atlantic Ocean. This small island of nine square miles has a year-round population of less than three thousand. Assateague, a barrier island, spreads its sandy arms around her full length, protecting her from the Atlantic.

I was introduced to Chincoteague when I read *Misty of Chincoteague* as a child. The story of the wild ponies of Assateague Island and the Beebe family made such a deep impression on me that when Gene and I wanted to get away for a few days, I suggested to him we go to Chincoteague. He agreed, and off we went.

With high hopes and great anticipation, the eastern sky opening before our eyes, we crossed the causeway to find, not the Chincoteague of my imagination, but an island wounded, in intensive care, and in the process of being patched up after the devastation of a storm a decade earlier. The Ash Wednesday storm of 1962, as it came to be known, had not received any attention in the mountains of Pennsylvania where I was a senior in college. Ten years after the storm, we were disappointed to find limited lodging and a primitive wharf side eatery. It was a depressed and depressing place made more so by the fantasies I had entertained for twenty-five years. We couldn't wait to get out of town. In search of bright lights and excitement, we found a lovely motel with an attractive bar and restaurant in Salisbury, Maryland, and returned home the next day, leaving thoughts of Chincoteague far behind.

During the 1970s and '80s, wanderlust was never far below the surface for us. We had built two houses and were living in the second. Off and on for twenty years, we thought about moving. Missouri, Maine, Vermont offered the rural life we thought we wanted. In the early 1980s, Gene brought up fond memories of North Carolina where he had been stationed as a Marine, and we decided to take a trip there to see if his old memories would fare better than mine had with Chincoteague.

On the way to North Carolina, our car's muffler came loose near T's Corner on Route 13 in the Virginia portion of the Delmarva Peninsula. Informed that the nearest garage was in Chincoteague, we headed there. We arrived at George Hall's auto repair shop late Friday evening to learn that no work could be done on the car until Monday. The nearest auto parts store was located in Salisbury, fifty miles away. We grudgingly looked forward to being stuck in Chincoteague for three days and resigned ourselves to the delay.

What a striking difference ten years had made. We found nice lodging and, since we were without a car, walked the streets. We found friendly people, quaint shops, and appealing restaurants. The peace in the air was palpable. By the time the car was ready to roll, we were smitten. We did go on to North Carolina for a few days, but Chincoteague had captured our hearts, to remain not far from our thoughts.

During this time, we sold our second house and were living in the third we had built. We had always wanted a house on the water, and with money to invest, we began to look at properties on the Jersey shore. Nothing pleased us. What to do? Chincoteague? Is it possible? We began to work with several realtors in the area, which necessitated a few shopping trips to the island. Gene liked several of the properties in the interior of the island, which he was ready to buy.

"But, Gene, I want a house on the water."

"But, Bob, we can buy a house on one of the backstreets for a lot less money than waterfront."

"Listen, Gene, we already own one house not on the water. I want waterfront, or I'm not interested. Besides, there's a limited amount of waterfront on the east coast. It's a good investment."

And so we went, back and forth. At the end of yet another fruitless day of looking at property, we returned to the Island Motor Inn which offered a private deck overlooking the Inland Waterway with every room.

"Why don't we just live here for a couple years and forget about a house," I said, opening the paper. Then something caught my eye:

> Waterfront. Charming 2-story waterman's cottage, 2 bedrooms, 2 bath, enclosed porch. Also Shad Shack, Dock, Mobile Home and Bunkhouse

"Gene, this is it! It's just what we're looking for!"

"Who's the realtor, Bob? It's not yet five, why don't you call them."

Richard, the broker, was the only person left in the office.

"I'll meet you at 787 South Main in twenty minutes."

It turned out he knew nothing about the house, and the listing agent was unavailable. That didn't matter. This was it. Our eyes looked beyond the neglect, the tasteless overcrowding of rooms, the windows hidden behind a triple layer of aluminum blinds, curtains, and heavy brocade drapes. We focused on her potential, possibility, and location, location, location. Within the hour, we signed the contract.

We went home full of optimism to await the closing. There were a few bumps along the way. The house had no heat. New Jersey novices that we were, a house without heat had never occurred to us. There were plumbing problems. We accepted it all because we were in love with her. A lover, wild about her beloved, knows she can overcome anything, and we were crazy about her. A few days before

Christmas 1986, we traveled to Chincoteague to take possession of our sweetheart. We were as happy as if we were welcoming a new baby into the family.

We spent the next three years going to Chincoteague almost every weekend, each time not wanting to leave. Our families, our entire lives had been in New Jersey, but no longer was our heart there.

It wasn't easy in 1990 to leave two newlywed daughters, family, and friends, but the call to live on Chincoteague Island was too strong to resist. Gene's diagnoses of kidney cancer ten years earlier, and the awareness of his mortality was never far from his mind. Cancer seems to be a malevolent disease, which is accompanied by a harassing *spirit* that never fully goes away. In addition, he loved to fish and had always wanted a boat. Even if I did not love Chincoteague, where life was lived with friendliness and care like I was accustomed to growing up; even if I had not always wanted a home on the water; even if I didn't love the beach—I would have been compelled to move for no other reason than if Gene died and I prevented him from his dream, I would have not been able to live with myself.

Everybody thought we were crazy. We were going off to start a new life at forty-nine and fifty-three with no job or prospects. Reckless as teenagers, we had $600 to our name. Oh, yes, we had assets, but grocery stores are not kindly disposed to accept assets. Uncle Walt was worried.

"You don't know where you're going or what you're going to do," he told us as we left New Jersey.

Two weeks later that summer, he died suddenly of a heart attack, leaving on a trip far exceeding ours in mystery. Back to New Jersey we went, carrying our condolences to Aunt Carol, my favorite aunt, who wore heartbreakingly sad eyes over the loss of her partner of fifty years. We returned to Chincoteague a few days later and settled in, not crossing the causeway again until Christmas.

Considering our precarious financial situation, we had no idea how long we would be able to stay, but I was hoping for at least one year to experience the four seasons. If we were unable to make a new life, we could always go back to New Jersey. We still owned the house that had failed to sell.

We bought business cards and put an ad in the phone book. "Gene Fusco Plumbing Service," was officially open for business. I spent weeks waiting by the phone, ready to direct Gene to the latest plumbing emergency. Meanwhile he was out and about, meeting the local tradesmen and picking up work water-piping new construction on the mainland. He made friends with Mr. Showard—the owner of the hardware store—who told do-it-yourselfers who found themselves in over their heads to call Gene Fusco. Gene's likable personality and integrity won him many friends, supporters, and customers.

We were warned, "If you're a 'come here,' they'll never accept you." "If a cat had kittens in an oven, it don't make 'em biscuits, do it?" Why, I know someone brought to the island as a week ole baby and was never accepted as a Teager. These warnings seemed not apply to us. We were accepted as much as we wanted to be.

A few months after settling in, Jeanne—our older daughter—bought us an answering machine, which freed me to go to the beach or walk the streets and get acquainted with the shop owners. That November the weather was mild, and we enjoyed a lot of time on Assateague Island, Gene surf fishing and me walking for miles. I collected shells and used them to make picture frames and decorate wreaths. Tourist season was over, and we spent a quiet time waiting for clients. It was like an extended vacation. We enjoyed it and were free from worry.

Little by little Gene's business grew, and I received two commission checks from New Jersey real estate deals that had closed after we moved. We were surviving. I got a job in an art gallery, which was located in the front rooms of the owner's home. I was their first employee. Being in the gallery and meeting interesting people reignited my interest in art. I became good friends with the owners, Jonathan and Regina, who encouraged me in my artistic endeavors. I began painting again, something I had not done for twenty-five years, and began making jewelry—all of which sold in the gallery. A conscientious employee, I treated the shop as if it were my own. Roots were being put down as our place in the community unfolded.

Daily we were awed by glorious sunsets viewed from the dock or curled in the comfort of white wicker chairs on the front porch.

Cooking and other domestic chores were cast aside in order to see the show. Each evening sky—special, unique, one of a kind—never became stale or boring.

A wealth of shorebirds enchanted and delighted: oystercatchers, stilts, turnstones, and gulls of every type. Late fall brought flocks of babbling brant geese making their annual trip from their birth in the Arctic tundra to winter along the coast from Massachusetts to North Carolina. With the following spring came the raucous call of laughing gulls, signaling their migratory return. Ritual mating on every dock on South Main filled the air with sounds of wild orgasmic bliss. The rookery's continuous hum in the marsh grass a quarter of a mile across the bay greeted our predawn rising. Silent flocks of brown pelicans brought smiles and a reminder of my childhood delight in the limerick:

> A funny bird is the pelican,
> His mouth can hold more than his bellican,
> He can take in his beak
> Food for a week
> And I can't see how the hellican
> (Attributed to Dixon L Merritt and/or Ogden Nash)

On Assateague Island, white egrets would often roost in the tall pine trees looking, like giant Christmas tree ornaments. Great blue herons, glossy ibis, swans, and ducks of countless varieties filled the protected waters. Sanderlings and sandpipers scurried along the surf's edge, keen-eyed, searching for food.

The marsh grasses were captivating with their panoply of changing colors—bright spring green, dark green, autumnal gold, rust, red, and winter brown. The weather, fickle as a damsel besieged by a multitude of suitors, brought brilliant glaring sun, skies of azure, lapis, and cerulean. In contrast the sun was often camouflaged by multilayered clouds of many shades of gray. Storms bearing lightning, thunder, and pounding rain raced toward us out of the west across the five-mile wide bay. Nor'easters at times left us without a speck of dry land in sight.

One in particular caused me to quip, "Gene, I've always wanted to live on a houseboat but really would have preferred one with a rudder." We laughed, full of delight and wonder, living a life close to nature.

Year round, daily traffic in front of our house consisted of whining engines as boats chugged down the channel carrying local fishermen out to their most lucrative fishing spots. In the predawn darkness, large brightly lit commercial fishing boats created a beautiful picture heading for open seas.

In summer many pleasure boats dotted the bay, as well as pontoon boats taking tourists on excursions to see wildlife and the famous Chincoteague ponies. Campers of every description passed by on their way to Tom's Cove or Inlet View campgrounds. An endless parade of joggers, walkers, bikers, photographers, and plein air artists routinely enjoyed the sights and the smells of the outdoors. Each moment brought a different treasure to stimulate our senses and our imagination.

In winter stillness and quiet reigned. We were the sole year-round residents on our block, and I loved it—many houses, few people—the perfect town for me! Gene, more social than I, had his customers and his barroom buddies, many of whom were retired military who provided him more companionable friendship than he had experienced back home. Known as Gino, he was always ready with a few jokes. To this day, his memory invokes smiles.

Our neighbor was Elsie Beebe, the sister of Grandpa of *Misty of Chincoteague* fame. Talk about a book coming to life! According to legend, the ponies of Assateague Island got there when a Spanish galleon, on which they were being transported, sank and the ponies swam to shore. Although it is more likely local farmers kept their cattle and horses on Assateague, which provided natural fencing by water, the legend lives on. Each July, the locals, the saltwater cowboys, round up the herd and swim them to Chincoteague where the foals are auctioned off at the local carnival. It was a big event in the days before TV and all the electronic diversions we now have.

Although the story of the horses, I loved, and the close-knit family of Paul and Maureen Beebe brought me here, the water kept me. There has never been a time I can remember when I didn't know that I wanted to live by water. It is a mystery why this daughter of lion and sun has forever been attracted to water like metal fillings to a magnet. Childhood summers at Point Pleasant or at my aunt's beach house in Manasquan on the Jersey Shore were times I wanted never to end. Boardwalk and honky-tonk were never the appeal, but the magnificent endless sea with its crashing waves providing a ceaseless present heartbeat. High tide, low tide. Life in motion. The sea was an ever-present reminder that although we humans devote our lives attempting to create stability, that life—real life—is not static.

In addition to the sheer beauty of the sea, there is a physical, biological, chemical attraction to water. Science tells us that moving water, oceans, rivers, waterfalls, and storms generate an excess of negative ions—which energize us and lift our mood to give us a sense of well-being. The negative ions can benefit our health by bonding to free radicals. This might be an unconscious factor in the desire of the multitudes of people who seek healing in hot springs, mineral waters, and holy sites like Lourdes.

I don't know if my own attraction to water can be explained in scientific terms. All I know is the attraction is a reality that has woven itself throughout my entire life, from my childhood experiences at the shore, to my solitary times during college by the Delaware River, to my adult explorations of waterfalls and rivers. Moving to Chincoteague completed my search. I was living on the water. I was home at last.

Sometime during our first year, Gene said, "Bob, we need to find a church."

"Why? We haven't been going to church for a long time in New Jersey, so why here?"

I don't remember the rest of the conversation, but I began searching the paper for churches. On the island, there were Methodist, Baptist, Roman Catholic, and Church of God churches but no Episcopal church. We visited the Methodist Church, an attractive stone building with red doors. Architecturally, it reminded me of Saint George's Episcopal, where we were married. We were invited to a hymn sing with the Baptists, which was a lot of fun. No future for us in the Catholic Church as we would have to convert in order to fully participate. It seemed there was no church for us. Back to the newspaper.

"There's an Episcopal church at Jenkins Bridge on the mainland. Where in the world is that?"

"Well, Bob, I think we should find out."

Hindsight, as they say, is twenty-twenty, for it has taken me years to realize Gene's sensitivity and intuition. He knew I needed the church when I didn't have a clue.

One Sunday morning, off we went in search of Jenkins Bridge. We discovered a small community located on Holden's Creek, home to Emmanuel Church. It turned out to be sixteen miles from our home. Situated in the country surrounded by fields of soybeans, corn, and wheat, the small white church with welcoming red doors appealed to us immediately. Our first Sunday there happened to be the bishop's visitation for confirmation. Warm welcomes descended upon us, and during the service, I was convinced that this was where I belonged. A reception followed the service, which reminded me of Saint George's with its cucumber sandwiches, silver tea service, and lovely women bustling about looking to be of service. Although I did not know it at the time, this little congregation was to be a major factor in my rootedness on the Eastern Shore.

Within months I was asked to be a lay reader, and soon I began leading a Bible study. I served on the vestry and was senior warden. When our priest died suddenly of a heart attack, I was in New Jersey, where I had stayed after the Christmas holidays.

Gene had returned to Chincoteague and called with the news, "Bob, David died, and everyone's calling here, wanting to know what to do."

I rushed home and began encouraging the congregation as we faced not only the loss of a pastor but the resignation of the organist and the dying of an old organ.

People kept asking, "What are we going to do, we've lost everything."

"We'll be fine," I said. "Even though we've lost these things, we still have God, or more accurately, God still has us."

I began leading worship services, writing sermons and arranging for supply clergy. I enjoyed many fine meals while getting to know parishioners in their homes. But I'm jumping ahead here. On that first day, all I knew was that I belonged there.

We were planting roots, had many friends, and were financially solvent. To our delight, we had been able to enjoy our first round of four seasons. We were here to stay.

Our family refers to the next few years of our life as the "Camelot" years. They were a time of new life for us—a time of exploring, enjoying, creating, and experiencing new things about ourselves and our world. In spite of my enjoyment of all this wonder, Gene seemed to begin to lose interest. For example, when I wanted to go to Key West for our thirtieth wedding anniversary, he didn't want to go. We had no celebration. Our lives became dreary. His life consisted of work, drinking with his buddies at the Poney Pines or VFW or AJ's, and always, the never-ending television. He was in a rut, and a rut is nothing but a grave open at both ends.

I tried to encourage him, "This is our time. Let's enjoy it. So many people our age are raising grandchildren or are responsible for old parents. We're not. We're free. There are no guarantees how long this freedom will last. We should take advantage of it while we have a chance."

But he was unmoved. I should have known something was wrong. After all, as long as I had known him, this was the man who was always fantasizing moving somewhere or dreaming up new business ventures. He had owned a garage, F&M Service Center in Jamesburg, New Jersey. After that was sold, he began dreaming of a fish store, Gene's Fish and Clam Bar. Then Gene Fusco Plumbing Service. I think he suspected something was wrong too. But what? What was the problem?

The answer came in March 1997.

March–April 1997

March 27, Thursday

Gene came home from work with a pain in his chest.

"I pulled a toilet and felt as if something ripped. I don't know what happened, but it's painful."

"Here, take some Tylenol," I advised.

After dinner, he settled himself in front of the TV, felt better, and we figured it would heal. The following day was Good Friday. I was scheduled to read the lessons at the noon service at church; after which we planned to leave for New Jersey to spend Easter with our children. When he wasn't home in time to leave for church, I went looking for him. I found him in the doctor's office. One look at his face pulled me under a tidal wave of dread. I saw death on his face. In that second, I *knew* he was going to die. I saw it coming. I did all I could to deny it. I rejected it, called it a liar, and railed against it. He was waiting to see the doctor and told me to go on alone as I needed to be at church. I drove the sixteen miles to church awash in tears, screaming and cursing. It's a wonder I didn't have an accident.

The Old Testament lesson I had been assigned to read was Genesis 22:1–13. It's the story of God requiring Abraham to go to the mountain, build an altar, and sacrifice his only son, Isaac. During the three-day walk in the wilderness, Abraham believed God would take his beloved son; but at the moment, he is ready to wield the knife God provides a ram for the sacrifice. Isaac is spared. I knew I had to be willing to offer up Gene, but would he ultimately be spared? When I arrived at the church, distress clothed my face. I choked my way through an emotional, throat-clenching reading.

Leaving church, I went back to the island to pick up Gene so we could head north.

"The doctor gave me some pills for the pain and an inhaler to help with the breathing. That's all he could do. He told me to go on to New Jersey for the weekend, but be sure to stop at Peninsula Regional for routine X-rays on the way home."

March 31, Monday

We knew Gene had a problem but, in spite of the feeling of impending doom, hoped the X-ray would diagnose the problem, he would get treatment, and everything would be okay. It was not to be. After the X-ray, I heard the words that shall be forever etched in my memory:

"Your husband has to be rushed to OR and have a chest tube put in to drain the pleural fluid. Every one we have seen like this is malignant. Don't you have family in New Jersey? I think you'd better go back there."

New Jersey? Absolutely not! Leave beautiful Chincoteague Island to hang out in New Jersey and wait for the Sword of Damocles. No. If Gene has any hope at all of survival, it's right here, at home.

I now was facing the unthinkable prospect of *we* becoming *me*. Life was tumbling upside down. Only twice in our thirty-four years of marriage had we been separated. In the early 1970s, he had flown to Oklahoma to attend the funeral of his brother's only child, David. I can still remember the lingering scent of his Mennen aftershave after he kissed his sleeping girls good-bye. (Laura, almost fifty, cherishes his last bottle—a reminder of watching him shave then cupping her face with Mennen-scented hands singing, Laura Beth Fusco, you little sweetie you.) Separated again in 1978, he was in hospital, having kidney surgery. Now he's in a hospital, fifty miles from home, ceaselessly pumping out pleural fluid, submitting to daily X-rays and countless endoscopes and biopsies.

Daily I make the early-morning drive to be with him and return to an empty house late every night. A few times, the hospital staff gives me an easy chair and I spend the night. I don't want to leave him, as if by my presence, I can protect him somehow. Friends who come to visit tell me I look like I'm the one who needs the hospital bed.

The multitude of tests reveal no cancer cells, and yet the pleural fluid won't stop draining. Uncertainty is a killer. One makes an attempt to deal with facts, but what can one do careening on the plane of uncertainty? We are confused. The doctors seem confused. High on morphine, after one test, Gene is again encouraged when no cancer cells are found in the pleural fluid.

"They didn't find any cancer. Isn't that great?"

"Yes, Gene, that's great, but it seems obvious to me that no matter what the cause, your condition certainly isn't normal, and it's not improving."

Drugged, he was unable to see the wisdom of my thinking.

I complained, "Why do I have to go through life cold sober, while you've always been able to get away with being drugged?"

My irritation had been fueled by his answers to the doctor's questions about his drinking habits. The admitted one or two drinks daily ultimately became eight to ten. He had told me over the years he had to keep working hard to take care of me, and now I learn he's been throwing money away over the bar to the tune of seventy drinks a week. Most of our marriage, I worried about paying bills. His carelessness with money, alcohol, and horse racing nearly brought me to divorce in the mid 1970's. Now, after years of self-destructive behavior, he's facing death.

It is my belief that alcoholism is subtle suicide. I had devoted years to studying nutrition and knew if you were destroying your body with alcohol, tobacco, or drugs that you should give serious attention to diet, exercise, and seek mental, spiritual health. That he had not done. I had read that the healing process of any addiction requires getting to the point where one is willing to forsake all external remedies to control feelings, thoughts, etc., and turn with absolute sincerity toward internal remedies—which are spiritual. Some addicts don't want to see or hear and have become callous in their self-centeredness and think only of their own comfort. The bottom line is that the rehabilitation process is a conversion process. I couldn't help believing he was killing himself. And I was angry about it.

In the midst of my heartbreak, anger, and fear, I looked to hold on to the one thing I knew was true. Thirty years earlier, I had gone through a time of severe disappointment that produced a deep hopelessness. In utter despair, I had cried out, "God, if there's a God, let me die. I can't live like this anymore." The murky memory of time clouds other details, but I rose up bathed in love. I *knew* God loved me. I knew God was real, more real than my own hand in front of my face. For months the sky was bluer, the grass greener, and a song thrummed in my heart. God became the love of my life, and I looked to him like the Israelites looked to the cloud and pillar of fire in the desert.

I had left my *Daily Office* book in the hospital for Gene, and each day we did Morning and Evening Prayer together. These times offered promise, hope, and security. In the book, he kept a picture of our cat and our grandson, Lucas Eugene, whom he adored. The pictures are still safely tucked between its pages to this day. Focusing on the reality beyond the medical model brought a balance into our lives, which would have been missing otherwise.

One morning, before leaving for the hospital, I came across a meditation by F. B. Meyer on Daniel chapter 3, which gave me a lot of encouragement. It goes like this: while in captivity in Babylon, Shadrach, Meshach, and Abednego refused to deny the God of Abraham, Isaac, and Jacob by worshipping an idol. Their punishment was to be thrown into the midst of a burning fiery furnace, to which they replied, "If that is the case, our God whom we serve is able to deliver us."

King Nebuchadnezzar then ordered them to be bound from head to foot and thrown into the fire—a fire so hot that the flames killed the men who threw them in. Upon looking in the fire, the astonished king asked his advisers, "Did we not throw three men bound into the midst of the fire?"

They affirmed that was so, to which the king replied, "I see four men loose, walking in the midst of the fire, and they are not hurt, and the form of the fourth is like the Son of God."

The message I got from Meyer's meditation was, "Don't fear the fire. It will set you free. It will work out for your good."[1]

Every day Gene and I walk the corridors, unable to go outside to smell fresh air or watch trees flutter in the breeze. We couldn't hear sweet birdsong or feel the sun bathing our skin. I don't know how he tolerated the isolation from nature because every night at nine or ten o'clock, as I left the confines of the hospital, I raced the fifty miles home, breaking every speed limit and inhaling any air that wasn't hospital air. I clearly remember sitting at the end of our dock, soaking in the comfort of the night sky, the stars in their courses, and the lap, lap of the water against the pilings. In the midst of feeling that my world was falling apart, I found stability there for a time. As I lifted my eyes to the heavens, looking for hope, looking for medicine for my breaking heart, I would be overwhelmed with God's love and uplifted in joy.

* * * * *

---

1. There was no doubt about their being bound. Whatever else the fire could not do, it at least freed them so that they walked loose. This is what trials have often done for us. We had become conscious of the binding effect of our own habits, but gradually the conviction grew that they were the weights that should be laid aside. Yet they clung to us until some fiery trial befell us, and from that hour, through the grace of the Holy Spirit, we were free. Do not fear the fire. Jesus never allows his beloved to walk the fire alone. If it is heated seven times hotter than is wont, this is only the reason for his becoming more real as our living and glorious Friend. There always goes beside the tried saint another whose aspect is that of the Son of God. (Our Daily Homily, F. B. Meyer in The Spirit-Filled Bible, NKJV)

When the pleural fluid does not stop draining, a pleurodesis is done. This is a procedure that entails talc administered through the chest tube, which seals the pleural lining and stops the draining of fluid.

When I ask what the long term effects of this procedure are, I receive not an answer, but a look of incredulity, as if I were an idiot. Medically speaking, there is no long term scenario. The day following this procedure, which permanently stopped the drainage, Gene is free to leave the hospital. But when the time comes for discharge, the doctor is out having a pizza and can't be found to sign the release form. Stretched to the limit by this last straw, I tell the nurses, "Look, my husband has been here for sixteen days, and he's leaving! There is nothing the doctor can do for him. I am taking him, with or without your permission!"

I wheel him out and put him in the car. I have sprung my prisoner!

On the way home he says to me, "If I die, you'll get married again. You're a good-looking woman."

"Are you out of your mind? Once is enough!"

More importantly, he said, "If I live, I love God, if I die, I love God."

Total acceptance. A whole lot better than I was able to manage.

Across the causeway, home at last—familiarity, peace, and routine, the illusion of being in control. We embark on a period of deep, meaningful communication and enjoyment of one another. I read books to him while we sit on the porch. We talk. We talk about our past, our dreams, our family, and our hopes for them. He confesses he's been too busy, too mentally preoccupied, to truly see and enjoy this lovely place. We are as close as we had been at the beginning of our life together.

"Now that you've come back to me, I'll be really pissed if you die and leave me."

Problems draw us into an orphaned and isolated state where we are driven to consciousness. The Biblical fall of man presents the dawn of consciousness, knowing good and evil, as a curse that separates us from the paradise of unconscious childhood. We want simple smooth lives of certainty, but certainties arise only through doubt, and result only through experiment. Blessed are those who are drawn to consciousness rather than driven.

—Carl Gustav Jung, 1875–1961
Founder of Analytical Psychology

Hanging On

"Blessed are those who are drawn to consciousness rather than driven."

I am driven, not drawn, as I watch Gene grief-stricken over the probable loss of his life. I want to save him and take away this awful death sentence.

I complain to God, *How could you let this happen? I don't understand how you could do this to him. I wouldn't wish this on my worst enemy.*

After we were so very close upon his return from hospital and were more in love with one another than we had ever been, I can't bear the thought of losing him. I am hanging on for dear life. I refuse to let him go. I am filled with anguish, watching him clear out the building where his plumbing supplies are stored, grief and sorrow written in every move of his body. Some of the materials are bought back by the supply house. Some he gives away.

I go for long walks on the beach, screaming, sobbing into the wind and waves that I hope will muffle the sound of my grief.

"No, no, no," is my mantra. "This is wrong. This is not right. This can't be your will."

I am a willful spiritual toddler in the terrible twos, resisting the present reality in internal temper tantrums. I am hanging on to Gene's life and our former life and refusing to go down the road ahead.

29

After all, I know God's will, don't I? Gene had been healed in a most dramatic way eighteen years earlier, following a diagnosis of a malignant tumor in his left kidney. On August 28, our sixteenth anniversary, I was told he needed surgery, followed by cobalt and chemotherapy—which might, just might, give him a fifty-fifty chance of survival.

With life and death before me, I had left the hospital praying, "They that are against us are so many; open thy servants eyes" (2 Kings 6:16). I wanted sight. I wanted reassurance. It was not meant to be—for me, that is.[2]

At hospital the next day, when I saw Gene, these were his first words, "Bob, what does God look like?"

As if I ought to know. He went on to tell me he'd had a visitation. Someone with hair like fire had stood in front of him, wearing a stern, fierce expression, looking not at Gene but over his left shoulder at *something*. Who was this? God? The Archangel Raphael? Another messenger of healing? We don't know. What we do know is following the surgery, we were told the tumor was encapsulated, and Gene could look forward to sporting a major scar at the beach the following summer. He was released from the hospital five days later, with no follow-up care. It was truly a miracle for us. I believed the same thing could happen again.

The healing in the hospital was soon to be followed by another miracle. I had come home from work one day to Gene.

"We're selling this house."

I could hardly believe my ears.

"Praise the Lord. Glory to God. Hallelujah," I shouted as I ran to get my Bible.

I couldn't wait to show Gene notes I had been saving for over a year and a half, words from God: "In 1981, you will sell this house and hold the mortgage, which will give you a monthly income, you

---

2.   In 2 Kings, Elisha's servant says, "They that are against us are so many." And Elisha tells him not to be afraid for "those who with us are more than those who are with them." Elisha prays, "Open his eyes, Lord, so that he may see." After that, the servant sees the heavens filled with chariots and warriors.

will build a smaller house on the adjoining lot. The future sale of that house will be your retirement." Gene was shocked—absolutely wowed. We immediately put the house on the market, and in less than twenty-four hours, it was under contract. I began drawing up plans for the "house of promise."

The "house of promise" was a sign and symbol of Gene's new life and the power of God. Our daughters had more years with their father. We eventually moved to Chincoteague. He was able to welcome his two grandchildren into the world. Why wouldn't, why couldn't, God heal him again? I believed the scriptures, knew every one of them that promised health and salvation. I had built my life on them. The proof that Jesus was doing the will of the Father was he healed those who came to him. My resistance, my stubbornness, my refusal to admit defeat was founded on the Word of God.

I knew I was right.

Not only was my theology right, I had accumulated a lot of anecdotal evidence from other sources over the previous thirty years. There were authorities in the scientific and medical world who confirmed my beliefs—Bernie Siegel, MD, for instance. He practiced surgery in New Haven and taught at Yale. In 1978, he started ECaP (Exceptional Cancer Patients), a specialized form of individual and group therapy based on "carefrontation"—a loving, safe, therapeutic confrontation that facilitates personal change and healing. Working with this group, he learned that the key to recovery lies in connecting with the emotional roots of the illness. This discovery led to his desire to make everyone aware of his or her own potential for healing and in 1986, published, *Love, Medicine, and Miracles: Lessons Learned about Self-Healing from a Surgeon's Experience with Exceptional Patients.* Because of his teachings and beliefs, he had been accused by his peers of offering false hope.

"False hope?" he counters. "What about those of you who give false despair?"

Another was Larry Dossey, MD, the author of *Healing Words,* which I read when it was released in 1993. He advocated the role of the mind in health and the role of spirituality in health care and has authored eleven other books on the subject.

A scientific authority who made a lasting impression on me was Candice Pert, a neuroscientist who worked at National Institutes of Health for one year and the National Institute of Mental Health for twelve. I saw her on the Bill Moyers 1993 PBS special *Healing and the Mind*.

Near the conclusion of the interview, he said to her, "Oh, what you are talking about is mind over matter."

"No, I'm talking about mind *in* matter."

Her *Molecules of Emotion* and *Everything You Need to Know to Feel Go(o)d* are fascinating reads. These are just three of the hundreds of doctors, scientists, psychologists, and philosophers who—though not professing religious belief—confirm what the scriptures had taught me. I thought I had a lot of evidence to support my belief that Gene did not have to die, and I wasn't going to give up without a fight.

Since the tumor in Gene's lung was inoperable, he chose to have chemo. Taxol was considered a potent choice in the battle against lung cancer even though it predicted a fifty-fifty chance of giving him only a few extra months. He, being the patient—deafened by shock and fear—was grasping at straws. Never a fan of chemo, these odds didn't appeal to me, but it was his life, his choice, not mine.

The treatments consisted of intravenous infusions at the oncology office at Peninsula Regional Hospital in Salisbury, Maryland, over the course of eight hours once a month, five months in all. Gene felt quite normal after the first two, and we were told X-rays indicated a shrinking of the tumor. Encouraged, we continued. I had great hopes for his recovery until July, when he began to experience the side effects of hair loss, tiredness, weakness, loss of appetite; and these symptoms convinced him that the doctor's original death sentence was true. He surrendered to the word of the doctors. After the final Taxol treatment, we were told the X-rays were impossible to read. They couldn't tell tumor from scar tissue from pleural fluid. This made no sense to me. How could the reading a few months earlier be accurate and now the doctors couldn't decipher what they're looking at? Still, I prayed and believed for healing, but Gene could not throw off the power of the white coats. As I focused on Gene, trying to instill him with hope, trying to get him to live, I became miserable because of his inability to receive the positive.

Ultimately, I realized no matter what happened to him, I needed to live, to be well, and I decided to begin a process of deep psychological and theological exploration. I started recording stream of consciousness thoughts in my journal, a technique recommended by many therapists.

In reading *Healing and Wholeness* by John Sanford, a Jungian psychoanalyst and Episcopal priest, I began to see I had focused on Gene our entire married life. *And why, God, did I do that?* I wondered. The answer was swift in coming, "Because you felt he was responsible for your happiness. You felt you were no longer captain of your own ship. After a number of years of marriage, when you realized you were tied at the hip with an addictive, self-destructive person who walked on the edge of a cliff, you believed if he went over, you'd go over with him. It has taken the hell of cancer to prove to you that is a lie. You are tied to the Holy Spirit, who will never let you fall."

Insightful, encouraging words, but I was deeply entrenched in the old habits, and change was slow in coming. I knew I had to let him go, but I continued being frustrated, impatient, and angry with his passivity. Alternately, I wallowed in pity for him—unproductive attitudes and contrary to who I wanted to be. I was between a rock and a hard place. On the one hand, I was trying to let him go. On the other, I felt if I stopped hounding him, feeding him, caring for him, and left him alone, he would die, and I would be responsible and guilty for the rest of my life.

Letting Go

Convinced my sanity and any life worth living depended on letting Gene go, I finally was willing. Fortunately, I found a book by Thomas Hora, MD, a psychiatrist who had been inspired to go beyond conventional medical practices to find healing of illnesses and mental disorders. He gradually demonstrated that the solutions to all problems were to be found in the realm of the spiritual. His book, *Beyond the Dream*, presented ideas that resonated with me, and this new perspective enabled me to begin to let Gene go. I saw that the way to let God help me was to turn my interest away from the problem. I needed to replace self-reliance with God-reliance, which involved just "letting be." "Letting" is what we allow to happen when we are consciously aware that God is the only power and is always in control, regardless of appearances to the contrary. "Letting" can't be done by us, only "letting go."

I also read that aggressiveness and passivity are two sides of the same coin because both are ways of ignoring the power and presence of God. It was a lightbulb moment when I admitted that Gene, the passive, and I, the aggressive, were the same. We were both ignoring God. I became willing to stop fighting with cancer and focusing on Gene. I determined to hold still by God's grace, to adopt an attitude of praise, and to give thanks in all things. I chose to stay in the fire. This was not an easy nor a rapid change. The choice was followed by emotional extremes of sorrow, anger, and grief that contrasted sharply with hope, love, and joy.

Looking for insight wherever it could be found, I walked to a neighbor's house where she was offering a study on temperaments. After taking the tests, it seemed that I was a strong-willed choleric—which meant, on the positive side, I was determined, visionary, goal-oriented, and self-disciplined. Contrarily, my negative side was expressed as a cold, unforgiving person who refused to admit defeat. I was definitely living in the negative. I recognized Gene as the loveable, charming sanguine—whose negative side was egocentric, undisciplined, and weak-willed. His inability to keep resolutions led to his need for immediate gratification. Since under stress, we regress. We had both regressed, and he drove me nuts—especially now that he was fighting for his life, or not fighting, as the case may be.

*****

Into the midst of all this "Sturm and Drang" came a delightful gift. We had a large garden about twenty-by-sixty feet, and this summer in particular, it was a source of comfort and refuge. I would go out at dawn before the heat of the day to weed a little and check to see if the deer had spared the Zucchetta Rampicante, a light green, long, curved squash which was my pride and joy.

One morning I hear a loud squawking above my head. No seagull was this. I look up to see a parrot buzzing me. I am perplexed and enthralled as parrots definitely are not indigenous. He returns the next day, and the next. I am delighted as, in Red Baron fashion, he strafs me with his piercing squawks. He is a delight to behold. I believe he has chosen me to befriend, and I promptly name him Verdi for his brilliant green color. I buy parrot food, and every day he comes to the porch railing to eat, He is a pleasure to watch as he tilts his head, grabs the seed with one claw, and raises it to his vivid red beak.

Often while he is eating on the porch, the hummingbirds who returned every year would circle him, staring, as if to say, "What are you doing here?"

I don't know how he knew where my bedroom was, but every day at daybreak, he'd perch on the roof of the house next door and screech at my window to wake me. I had long desired to own a parrot, but having him in my life made me wonder if I could ever live with such a dominant personality.

I would be very upset when the neighbors came for a weekend with their barking dog and frighten Verdi off. Relief would come after they left when he returned to me and stayed while I sat and read and he ate.

As fall approached and the weather turned cold and windy, I began to worry about him. After all, he did live in the tropics, didn't he? Soon after he had arrived a friend had loaned me a cage, and I tried to entice him with food, to no avail. He refused to be trapped, and he never trusted me to touch him. Fearing the cold weather, and not wanting to lose him because he had brought me so much joy, I began to ask God why he had brought him to me, only to let me lose him. After a very cold night in early September, I was relieved to wake to his familiar squawking in the morning.

The third week in September, there was a lot of noise in the neighborhood, tourists, lawn mowing, and end-of-season yard work. Verdi was wary and nervous. Though he flew his usual patterns, he refused to settle on the porch and eat. Several days later, I returned home from running errands to find the cage had been picked up. All his routine had been upset. All my routine had been upset. And then one day, he was gone.

Why did he mean so much to me? Why did I love him, enjoy him, feel responsible for him? My husband was dying of cancer, and I was grieving over the loss of a parrot. Transference? I walked the neighborhood for days—blocks and blocks in every direction—looking for him, looking for green feathers, looking for a corpse. Nothing. Gone without a trace.

*****

Meanwhile, John, my best friend's husband, died of prostate cancer. We made plans to attend his funeral in New Jersey, and Gene was very down as he pondered what could be his future. Consciously, I felt quite stable, but underneath was a piercing sorrow. By the time of Verdi's disappearance and John's death, Gene had not recovered from the effects of chemo and began withdrawing into himself.

Gene constantly has the television on. I go to my bedroom to read, think, and pray. My home as I knew it is now gone. I go out and talk with friends, but that is tiring and only slightly better than being here with the constant TV. Now that fall is here and the crowds gone, I think I'll go back to walking on the beach every day.

I sometimes wonder if I am the most selfish, heartless, inhuman person in the world. Or is it that I know myself more intimately than I know anyone else? Last night was Mother Theresa's funeral. She loved attending to sick people. I don't. I really don't. God has been very generous to me, and yet I don't like sick people, or maybe it's that I don't like sickness. Maybe I don't know God at all.

The Word of God says, "I will rebuke the devourer for your sake."

Sickness is a devourer. It erodes your life, your relationships, your finances, your joy, and your optimism. It's a black hole—no, a black vortex—that seeks to suck all life into it. Jesus did the will of the Father, and he healed people.

You know, I really feel let down by you, God. When two enter the sacrament of marriage, they become one flesh. I ask you, how can I have cancer?

He said not, 'Thou shalt not be tempested,
thou shalt not be travailed,
thou shalt not be dis-eased;' but he said,
'Thou shalt not be overcome
—Julian of Norwich

Journal—
More Letting Go

September 14

Sweet breeze . . . Breath of God . . . Passing by . . . Unseen . . .
Revealed in gentle tones of contemplation . . . I love you, God.

September 15

Exhausted. Awake again at 3:00 a.m., thinking about chemo and
how I hate its debilitating effects and how I have no faith in doctors. After the second chemo treatment, they said the tumor had not
grown, so we continued treatment, and now they tell us they can't tell
fluid from scar tissue from tumor. Makes no sense to me.

September17

Awake at 2:00 a.m. I keep trying to find little spaces of routine in this
unsettled life with Gene. I feel as if I have no life. I'm drowning. I'm
being jerked around and eaten alive. I have no personal space except
now in the middle of the night with a gentle breeze, a full moon, and
night creatures.

September 24

I wake, remembering a dream of a beautiful large church where we were having our Emmanuel Jenkins Bridge Christmas Eve service. Guest musicians gave heavenly music. Rosamond wanted us to sing, and I refused to degrade these visitors with our lack of musicality. There was a priest, or angel, who assured me that he would see to it that Gene would die without suffering and without reproach. Both Gene and I know that if he lives, praise the Lord, and if he dies, praise the Lord, but we're both apprehensive concerning the time between now and then.

At Bible study last night, my dear friend Iris said that God had confirmed to her that Gene would be fine. She can't confirm a physical healing or a death of this body, but he will be fine. And now the spirit of the night confirms what she told me.

September 30

I begin giving Gene Restores, a natural supplement that is used in rehabs to help people get off drugs and alcohol and to relieve depression. He seems much more "alive." Two of them keep him awake all day, and he is more communicative. I give him two more. He complains they made him edgy and angry. Well, I had noticed. I tell him he's always been angry and just stuffed it. We had just listened to a radio program on depression, and he had said they were describing him to a tee. The Restores are helping him get in touch with his feelings. The question is, will he allow that to continue, or will he seek sedation again as alcoholics are prone to do? Will he see that by shutting off the negative emotions, he automatically shuts off the positive? Mind, body, spirit are connected, are one. He finally ends up refusing to take more Restores because they put him in touch with his emotions. He doesn't want to go there. When we were first married, I probed a lot till finally he told me he didn't want to know what was in there. At the time, I told him some people skate on the surface of life, and some are deep-sea divers. I am definitely a deep-sea diver. He didn't want to dive then. He doesn't want to dive now. Will he ultimately want to dive?

October

October 8

Gene's life consists of the TV and the couch. My life consists of water and sunsets on the front porch, books, and quiet in which to meditate. I entertain a bright idea to make the trailer, my former workshop, the TV "room." This idea gives me hope for our future, however long that may be.

Last night at church, Betty said, "You have a calling. What are you going to do about it?"

I was aware that I had been anointed to preach on Sunday, and she confirmed, "You could have heard a pin drop. Art was moved to tears."

October 13

Awake at 3:00 a.m. sorrowing, regretting, blaming. Go to the living room and sit by Gene without a word, mentally walking with him as a salt doll into the sea that is God (Archbishop Anthony Bloom's symbol of prayer). Be, just be. Some say the highest form of prayer is just letting God be, leaving the outcome in his hands. God is in the present, in the now, not in the past, nor in the future. I have, for too long, seen Gene as a black hole—always wanting, wanting, wanting. Wanting me to do, do, do. Get me this, get me that, a perennial toddler taking all in, giving nothing back out. *But*, am I not the same to him? Wanting, wanting a spiritual, emotional, mental response. Never being satisfied with what is, always wanting something more. He demands the physical. I demand the spiritual. Are we not both demanding something of one another that the other does not, cannot, or will not give? I could be sucking his life away as much as I feel he sucks mine. A draining psychic energy field exists between us. We need to just *be*.

October 21

The habit of thinking of what should or should not be tends to make us willful and tyrannical. This, in turn, can promote tyrannical and rebellious reactions. This is part of what goes on between me and Gene. We need to give up should for shouldlessness. Shouldlessness is thinking that's based in the nondual nature of God where everything is harmonious, intelligent, and very good. When we understand and affirm this, we have placed our problems into the hands of God, and things work out because God is the harmonizing power of the universe. When we get hooked into should/should not thinking, we can't see what is. Letting be is reverent, loving responsiveness to that which is from moment to moment. It is a spiritual, constructive attitude. It is not leaving alone. That is neglect. Ah, a fine line to walk.

October 23

The girls in the bank asked, "What did you used to do?" It got me to thinking. I have supported and undergirded Gene our entire married life, from the garage to the fish store to the plumbing business. What am I going to do now? Whether Gene lives or dies, I must live out the purpose for which I was born. I am a teacher, a preacher, a counselor. The year Jenkins Bridge had no priest and I was senior warden was the most rewarding year of my life. God enabled me to be and do things I never dreamed possible. I was blessed, and the congregation was blessed. Is my future ordained ministry?

November

November 2

Sunday. A happy day. A sad day. Happy, because Fr. Bill Starkey and a half dozen friends come to the house to celebrate communion with us in honor of All Saints Day. A sad day because Gene discovers he can no longer sing when the group begins singing *For All the Saints*.

He had a marvelous bass voice, and the loss of it grieves him and pierces my soul.

Late in the afternoon Gene gives me a most precious gift. We are facing one another across the dining room table, and I began to tell him that I have often felt responsible for his condition, because if I had not married him, he could have remained a happy, irresponsible bum. I was referring to his high school yearbook motto, "Pleasure is the business of my life."

The first three years of our marriage were a honeymoon. He had a job working shifts, which left time to go to the beach, fish, hug the babies, enjoy meals on the patio, and sleep in his own bed. But he wanted more. In an English-Scots-Irish town, his immigrant Italian family was at the low end of the social ladder. He grew up wanting to be *somebody*. His opportunity came in the form of my father, who told Gene of a garage in town for sale. He offered to put up money for a partnership in which Gene would be manager and my father would be silent partner. I'm sure my father wanted to provide the best for his little girl, but I was horrified. I pleaded with Gene to not get involved. I had firsthand knowledge of an absent parent and no family time when my father started his own business when I was a child.

He paid me no mind. The poor Italian kid, youngest of nine, teased because of his immigrant parents and big nose, asserted himself. He wanted to be a business owner. He wanted to be somebody. He had to do it. And thus, it was so. He was gone seven days a week—always on call when he was home, and my father, the silent partner, to Gene's distress, was not silent. The business chewed him up, and he began a walk down the path of psychic and physical pain. He never again found a comfortable bed.

When I finished, saying he would have had a happier life if we had not married, he said, "Bob, you did everything you could to talk me out of going into business with your father. You knew. You were right. My life went wrong when I tried to be 'somebody.' I remember well, you didn't want me to do it."

"Oh, God what a waste. I fell in love with you at the Gayspot when you were just a sexy playboy. I even called you Gino the gigolo. You didn't have to be anybody else for me. I loved you."

But of course, I realize he didn't do it for me but for the poor little Italian boy who was looked down on and shamed for being a guinea.

November 8

I have lived with a perception of myself as very realistic and unattached to material things. But during these trying months, I discovered that I have many dreams, fantasies, and attachments. I have found that I am holding on to a lot of would'abeens, coulda'beens, shoulda'beens regarding my marriage and my family. Daughter Jeanne put her house up for sale yesterday. She's leaving New Jersey and is moving to Arizona. Period. One year ago, I had eight members in my family. Soon, I shall have two. Jeanne is presuming on health and wealth to keep us all in touch. Big presumption. I am bathed in tears. God, grant me the grace to survive this storm of my life. My Gram was such a vital part of my life, and I will have no life with my grandchildren. God, you seem to be cutting me loose from every attachment except for Laura. May I learn to see this as not terrible loss but as great new freedom? But freedom for what?

November 12

We leave for New Jersey today to stay at Jeanne's house while she flies to Arizona.

November 14

At Jeanne Marie's in Robbinsville, New Jersey, I'm planning my day at 5:00 a.m. when it hits me: if I must plan things out, I am nervous and afraid and trying to protect myself from the pain that comes from being out of control, or from the pain of failing my responsibility to protect everyone. I've had a nervous stomach since I arrived because Gene is uncooperative and nonfunctional. Jeanne's cat, Jessie, will kill my cat if he gets near him. And I don't know the grandchildren Lucas and Bria well. It's up to me to keep everybody in order when the realtors come.

Gene had always planned ahead, so much so that he totally missed the "now." I have rarely planned ahead if I could avoid it. Maybe this panicky feeling is why Gene began planning. Now, maybe I can better empathize with him.

I ask you, Jeanne Marie, did you realize that you were leaving me with a dying man, two incompatible cats, and two children under the age of three who were basically unknown to me?

November 19

Returning from New Jersey after time with family and friends, I feel so alone I even want to leave Chincoteague, forgetting that I love it here. There is no escape from the pain of watching Gene. No escape. But a fundamental law of the Christian life is acceptance. Acceptance. But I keep seeking to escape, like a bird caught in a trap, and my only accomplishment is to break my wings even more painfully. They say it's always darkest before the dawn.

Where is that sunrise?

December

December 4

Oh, Gene, how I had hoped for years that you would meet me half-way in the little things of life, like turning off the TV before you went to sleep so that the late-night loud commercials would not wake me. I wake this morning crying inconsolably because the precious, sweet, good we once had will never be again, nor will the irritating lack of cooperation ever be minimized. I didn't realize the strength of the hope that we could become compatible in the daily round of life until that hope died. I woke with a terrible headache.

Oh, God, please preserve my life till Gene dies so that the girls are not responsible for him. Laura is doing so well at massage therapy school, and Jeanne is planning a new life in Arizona. I thank you for keeping me from expressing anger yesterday, but I think maybe my anger keeps me from the awareness of this terrible sorrow I'm feeling now.

December 15

Is it possible that Gene and others of his temperament—the nice, kind, self-controlled ones of the family—gave themselves cancer, and the screamers—the throwers of temper—are hale and hearty? I can see now Gene believed he had no choice, really. If he had given vent to his rage, he would have lost me and the girls, like Jeanne's husband lost her and his children. But as it is written, "He who saves his life shall lose it." There is a world of difference between stuffing your anger, your sin, trying to propitiate by self-punishment, *and* confessing it and accepting forgiveness.

December 16

Tuesday, an unplanned doctor's appointment to determine the cause of the severe retention of fluid. He looks like he would be in pain, but he isn't. Jeanne and Laura are coming Thursday. We all feel the time is short. I woke up this morning feeling so very sad.

Dear God, Jeanne and Laura will be here soon. Bless us this time together. Give us all peace. Enable Gene to give a blessing to his children. May we recognize and experience our oneness in you and your love. Amen.

December 18

Create in me, o God, the compassion of Christ, the ability to suffer with, the ability to live in the present moment —having no framework for my temporal life, with no plans, goals, or human hopes. I find I am so unable to live in the limbo of a living death or a dying life. I had believed I'd have no life unless Gene either got well or died, but around the periphery of my mind this morning, I feel you are calling me to really live in the midst of death. After all, isn't that what you do?

Results from the blood test on Tuesday reveal the Lasix isn't working because there's no extra fluid in his blood. The fluid can't get from the intercellular spaces to the bloodstream. I call Betty Leach, my nurse friend, and she recommends Epsom Salts, which she tells me was given to patients in hospital years ago. It pulls the fluid directly into the bowel, bypassing the bloodstream. She says it might help, and it can't hurt. Foul tasting, he took it and went from urinating once to three times every twelve hours.

December 30

Jeanne and Laura have gone back to New Jersey. The Epsom salts was a gift that worked to give them a nice time with their father. While they were here, he was more energetic, had a good appetite, and told a few jokes. But now they are gone, and he's refusing the salts. His chest on the right side is hugely swollen. Today is the day I know I have to get help. He needs a hospital bed, but I hate to get it and upset the grandchildren when they come on Saturday four days from now. He's failing rapidly. One month ago, he managed the flight of stairs in Laura's house, and now he can't get off the couch. My cat, Cecil, lies by me, eleven years in remission from feline leukemia—a living testament to the healing power of God. The Chrysler van sits outside the door with every option I ever wanted, which I take as a visible sign that God is looking to bless me. I have my dear home and so many other blessings. Will not God give us all things as blessing, though some are so easily recognized and some so heavily disguised?

December 31

I find Gene lying on the floor this morning. I feel completely helpless. Swollen with fluid, he is very heavy. Hospice is coming. I can no longer manage. Hospice is a godsend. Judy, the coordinator, comes at four o'clock and stays until eight o'clock when the hospital bed is delivered, and they get Gene into it. I no longer feel alone in this world. I can call them twenty-four hours a day. I no longer have to worry about him falling. He seems even quieter and more detached than he did yesterday. By his vital signs, the nurse tells me he has days, not weeks, left.

> There are years that ask questions and years that answer. (Zora N. Hurston)

We sure know which one 1997 was.

January 1, 1998

I descend the steep, high-riser, narrow tread steps to make coffee and check on Gene. He's safe now in the hospital bed hospice delivered last night. I had postponed getting the bed because he believed he would die once we got one. But after his fall yesterday, I had no choice. Unable to lift him, I had sat on the floor for a while next to him, crying in frustration at my helplessness. I had then called his friend, Chessie Rhodes, who operates a medical transport service. I knew he could get him up off the floor. Chessie brought several big strong guys, who got him back on the couch. They tried to persuade him to go to hospital. He refused, not wanting to prolong the inevitable. I concurred. As he was now safe in the hospital bed, I was at ease and had slept a few hours. Finding him sleeping peacefully at 3:00 a.m., I return to my bed, coffee, and faithful journal in hand.

I go back to the living room around six o'clock. He calls me, "Bob."

He always called me Bob.

"Can you move my pillow up?"

I attempt to do so. I arrange and rearrange the pillow several times. He seems frustrated with me. My knowledge of height, depth, and the four compass points is not serving me well. I mean, what is up? How many ups can there be? We go back and forth with our mutual frustrations, and in the midst of this controversy, he exhales and is gone. This breath is so easy, so peaceful, so natural, that I can't believe he is dead. Upon later reflection on this pillow incident, I believe he was beginning the journey, leaving his body, and therefore "up" was beyond my ken.

I call Judy Nock, the hospice nurse, who lives down county on the mainland about an hour away. Waiting for her, I sit with Gene, holding his hand. After reciting the Lord's Prayer, the Twenty-Third Psalm, and other prayers, I continue talking. I don't remember what I talked about. The one thing I do remember is that I continued to talk till I finally said, "This is like our entire marriage. I talk, and you don't answer."

I recall being amused by this noir humor.

The nurse arrives at last. She confirms that, yes, Gene is dead—really dead.

"What do you want to do now?" she asks.

"I want a cup of coffee."

We sit at the long, handcrafted table in the dining room, drinking our coffee and getting to know one another. She also was from New Jersey. Her husband, a painter, had worked on a house where Gene was replacing water pipes, and the two had developed a friendship. Her husband had died the previous year, also from lung cancer. She's the perfect person to accompany me during this difficult time. A sister in experience. A sister in loss. A sister in sorrow.

I call my daughters to give them the sad news.

Jeanne already knew. "I saw my father in the arms of an angel this morning."

Following that I called the funeral director, who arrived promptly. Then I began the task of calling friends and relatives. I had a few breaks during these conversations when my cordless phone lost its charge several times. Admittedly, this time is a blur, and I have few journal notes for a day or two.

It was evening before I wrote in my journal.

January 1

I write this date and sobs well up from my gut, convulsing my whole body. Went downstairs at five forty. Gene died at 6:00 a.m. Oh my god, bless my children and grandchildren in the New Year of so many changes. Bind cords of love around our hearts, and never let us go.

And now let us welcome the New Year full of things that have never been. (Rilke)

Most people have, at some time or another, to stand alone and to suffer, and their final shape is determined by their response to their probation: they emerge either the slaves of circumstance, or in some sense captains of their souls.

—Charles E. Raven

Emotional Land Mines

January

Just before Christmas, Gene had told me he wanted to be cremated and buried in the Good Shepherd Garden at Saint George's in New Jersey. I knew Roman Catholics had, for centuries, disapproved of cremation, so I was surprised at his decision, and I was also glad. We both felt it was fitting that his final resting place would be where we had been married and the girls had been baptized. It had been our church home for almost two decades, and some of our deepest friendships had been formed there. In addition, it simplified the funeral arrangements.

On Sunday, the fourth of January, prior to going to New Jersey, we celebrated Gene's life at Emmanuel Episcopal Church Jenkins Bridge. With the approval of Fr. Bill Starkey, I planned the service.

"You won't be pleased with it any other way", he said. How well he knew me.

He had been our supply priest ever since our vicar had died suddenly of a heart attack a few years earlier. As Senior Warden, I had run the church, finding supply clergy, planning worship services, and preaching my own sermons.

I knew the kind of service I wanted for Gene. I included his favorite hymns, "Holy, Holy, Holy" and "For All the Saints," and Fr.

Bill preached a meaningful, personal sermon. He knew Gene so well. There were many tears shed by all who had loved Gene's winning personality, his rich bass voice and tremendous sense of humor.

I was calm and did extremely well during the church service. Maybe God graciously was holding me until I went to New Jersey the following Sunday. Afterward, people told me they were waiting for me to break, but I remained cool and composed. The children had come to Virginia as soon as I told them Gene was gone, but on the day following the church service, Jeanne left for Arizona with her children and Mark, whom she married several weeks later.

"More painful to see them go than to have Dad die," Laura, my younger daughter, said to me.

That pain was a truth I was later to experience numerous times. It was a mild winter, and Laura and I walked arm in arm by the water as we looked for consolation in one another's presence.

The day after Jeanne left, Laura returned to her full-time job and to finish her training as a certified massage therapist.

Now I am alone.

I have no memory of the next day or two, and out of character, I have no journal entries. My friend Carol had given me *Simple Abundance*, a book that had been featured on Oprah's show. Finally, I opened it. The readings encouraged me to be grateful for all that I had. The glass is not half empty, but rather half full. The daily meditations helped me to focus on what I had, rather than what I had lost. Painful as it was, I was determined to follow the advice of Joseph Campbell, "We must be willing to get rid of the life we had planned, so as to have the life that is waiting for us."

My journal begins again two days after Gene's death.

January 3

I dream that Gene has died. It's settled. He's dead. I'm in a stainless steel surgical hospital area, and someone tells me they've taken Gene for a special surgical procedure to save his life. *How can they save his life? He's dead.* It turns out there's a scam whereby they do these surgeries for $10,000, knowing the person won't live.

"Where is recovery?" I ask.

Up. Up on the top floor. Many stainless steel steps. I come upon two dozen beds with post-op patients. I begin checking them, looking for Gene. I remember at this point that part of the scam was to kill any survivors with poisoned drugged ice cream. If he's alive, I have to save him. I find him lying in a fetal position on his right side. Alive. He responds to me. I had gotten there in time. I wake with a good positive feeling.

Twenty minutes after I wake, I close my eyes and can see him as clearly as in the dream.

"Gene, what have you to say to me?"

"Thanks, Bob, for finding me and getting here in time."

January 7

I am at peace. The peace of God rules in my heart. I am forgiven. I am accepting of God's will. If I accept the belief of some, whether true or not, that the day we die is fixed on the day we're born, then I can stop struggling with Gene and the choices he made. I can stop blaming him. I can let go of anger. After all, it is. And what *is*, is God's will for me.

January 8

Today is the one-week anniversary of Gene putting off corruption and putting on immortality. God bless him. May he go from glory to glory. I feel terrible he had to go through those nine months of hell. But I can't focus on that, or I shall fall into despair.

January 10

Yesterday was hard, very hard. I washed the van to go to New Jersey. I got very upset about Jeanne not being here for Gene's service at Saint George's tomorrow. I received a note from an old friend telling me how Gene had played a role in her becoming a Christian. Regret overshadows me.

He was a sweet man, and I gave him so much grief, begins my painful train of thought.

When I woke this morning, a residue of nighttime thoughts lingered in my mind:

Christ healed all who came to him. Was Gene unable to accept his healing? Or was the whole thing planned from the foundations of the world? Wrestle, wrestle, wrestle. *Stop it, Barbara! It no longer matters because today is what it is for you. This is the fact of your life now. How you got here is no longer the issue. What you do now is the issue.*

I pack the van and put in the container of Gene's ashes and drive him to New Jersey for the service at Saint George's in Helmetta on the eleventh. My six-foot, two-hundred-pound husband now in a twelve-by-eighteen-inch box. This has got to be the loneliest trip of my entire life. I pray for peace, assurance, and power in the Holy Spirit. I pray that Laura delivers her message about her Dad, with power, calm, conviction, and love.

It turned out this service was less meaningful to me than the one in Virginia. Yes, relatives and friends were present, but I had nothing to do with the planning, and the rector didn't know Gene or me at all. Except for Laura's talk, it was a far less personal affair.

I stay with Laura for over a week. I organize her closets and cupboards in a puny attempt to gain a feeling of control over life. Together she and I paint the living room, dining room, and the master bedroom.

Over the next few months, I go back and forth from Virginia to Laura in Jackson, New Jersey, all the while continuing my theological struggle.

January 17

I am tortured. It's as if I have two puzzle pieces that I am trying to fit—first one, then the other. If I rest on Psalms 91 and 103, which promise protection and healing, and if I believe all the teachers and ministers of healing now and in the history of the church, then I'm angry, because I believe Gene had a choice. For years, he danced with death.

How many times I had said to him, "If you go to a doctor and he says that you are sick, you will believe him completely. If he says you are well, you will believe him only until you have the next symptom or the next pain. You seem predisposed to believe the worst."

If, on the other hand, he had no choice, then he was a victim, and I am heartbroken. I go back and forth between choice<>victim, anger<>sorrow.

There must be another angle, another side, a puzzle piece that I have not yet found. I've got to stop tormenting myself with this. I find no acceptable answer. For a few days I find peace by accepting the premise that since God dramatically healed Gene in 1979, and Gene received that healing, then God and Gene could have done it again. Since it worked out the way it did this time, it must be God's will. I've got to accept it.

The weeks following Gene's death, the weather is as unsettled as I. January and February bring three nor'easters that wash away land behind my bulkhead and deposit a mountain of oyster shells in another area of the waterfront. When I leave Laura and go back to Chincoteague on Wednesday, the twentieth, I begin to spend days shoveling the waterfront mountain of shells into the valley of erosion. Indoors I clean and clear and organize. While painting the bathroom, rain and wind pound the old house and my soul. Is this a symbol of my life, I wonder. It feels like I'm rearranging the deck chairs on the Titanic.

January 24

Painful. I am entering a sad place, a tired place. Maybe I'm just worn out from nine months of trying to function for Gene and myself. Unlike all the ugly emotions of my previous journals, I feel I have little to say. In addition, the pain of watching my beloved cat get thinner and thinner, as his feline leukemia returns after a nine year remission, is the last straw.

It is so awful, watching someone die.

I fear now I will live my mother's life of loneliness and aloneness. She chose to leave my father the day Gene and I married. I was committed to keeping my marriage together, no matter the cost, and now I am alone anyway. Home has always been my priority, but a home without a family is nothing. I no longer need a house, but I don't want to end up in one room, like my mother did, either. Most of all, I don't want to burden Laura with my emotional needs. Some new widows have a settled home or a job or a family. My job was Gene Fusco Plumbing, and my family shrank from eight to two in the matter of a few days. I have no routine to return to. Gene was my life. Our business had taken a lot of time and attention. I am overwhelmed with not knowing where I want to live. In fact, I don't know anything.

January 24

Simple Abundance is right on today, "Bless a thing, and it will bless you. Curse it, and it will curse you. If you bless a situation, it has no power to hurt you." I make a list of all I am grateful for, from people to books to hot baths, and come up with one hundred items. I hope it helps.

January 25

Four a.m. Awakened by howling wind. I hate the wind. The rattles of the house. I am brought back to the night I left Gene in the hospital. When the wind roars, I just know I can't live here. But by five o'clock, I'm able to say with the Hebrews exiled in Babylon, blessed be the wind, blessed be the wind and all creation of God.

"If your everyday life seems poor, don't blame it; blame yourself; admit you are not enough of a poet to call forth riches; because for the creator, there is no poverty," Rainer Maria Rilke advises.

Praise the Lord of hosts, for the Lord is good. His mercy endures forever. Real gratitude begins when everything is falling apart. God, give me a grateful heart.

> Make my broken life a sacrifice
> Of praise to you
> Let not bitterness overtake me
> Don't let my enemies triumph

9:00 p.m.

Went to church this morning. Cried all through the service. Afterward had a lovely walk with Emily on the wildlife loop on Assateague. A day of contrasts.

January 28

I wake to another nor'easter. Yard underwater. Dear Gene, you know I have to get out of this precarious place. But where would I go on planet earth where there are no dangers? That's right. Nowhere. The few nights before you died, when I had no patience with you, haunt me. I cry out, please forgive me. Though I know you have. Where you are, you understand me more perfectly than I can understand myself. You know I love you, though I so poorly showed it. I know that you loved me. Thank you for sharing your life with me.

February

February 1

I lay on your altar, dear God, my total depravity. Enable me to accept your forgiveness for the way I attempted to battle Gene and his cancer in the flesh. I acted out in the flesh under the pain, strain, and fear of those last few months. I leave myself on your altar as a gift and hope to receive from you acceptance, love, and peace. Gene is your son. He gave his life to you. The ball is in your court, so to speak.

> I lay my Issac on the altar (Good Friday, March
> 28, 1997)
> I took him back many times
> I stayed with him in the wilderness
> I kept looking for the ram
> My eyes burned from my crying
> My throat ached from my screaming
> My chest pounded from my grieving

> I lay my Issac on the altar (December 24, 1997)
> God kept him . . . (Inspired by Genesis 22:1–13)

I will leave the wilderness, a treeless, waterless, burning, freezing place of devastating solitude.

But not today.

After two weeks of my own company, loneliness overcomes me, and I head back to Laura's. My cat Cecil is failing rapidly.

February 8

At Laura's. It's Resurrection day. Every Sunday. Oh, God, I feel like I'm back to square one in my sorrow. Had to put Cecil down yesterday on my way to Laura's. Even though his body was deteriorating, his spirit was mine. He was still responding to me in love till the bitter end. It's like Gene's death all over again. I hurt beyond words. I can't even bring him here to Laura's for burial. The ground is frozen solid.

I know why some widows go crazy, because I have a "hell with it, devil may care" attitude. To my son-in-law, I say, "So you want to go to Daytona to the races? Let's go. A good ticket is $500? So what. What's the difference?"

Unable to sleep, I get up at 2:00 a.m. in search of sanity. I must say the Venite.

> "Oh come let us sing unto the Lord
> let us heartily rejoice in the strength of our salvation.
> Let us come before his presence with thanksgiving
> and show ourselves glad in him with psalms.
>
> For the Lord is a great God
> and a great king above all gods.
> In his hand are all the caverns of the earth
> and the strength of the hills is his also.
> The sea is his and he made it
> and his hands prepared the dry land.

O come, let us worship and fall down
and kneel before the Lord our Maker.
For he is the Lord our God
And we are the people of his pasture
and the sheep of his hand.

O worship the Lord in the beauty of holiness;
Let the whole earth stand in awe of him.
For he cometh, for he cometh to judge the earth
and with righteousness to judge the world
and the peoples with his truth."

I must run to the rock of my salvation, for I am in a dry and barren land.

February 14

Back in VA. I can't live here. I have to sell the house. I start to paint the kitchen and hallway.

February 15

I am becoming acutely aware that there is no one in this world to whom I am most important. I have no one to stand between me and the world. In my reading, I am encouraged by this quote from *Night Watching* by Leslie Williams:

Undergirding each of our choices we make in life, God is leading us. In our ignorance or in our false desires we may make what we think is the wrong choice; however, because of God's redemption on the cross, there are no ultimate wrong choices. God redeems all our blunders, all our stupidity. The crucial choice is choosing God over not choosing God.

March

March 6

I was up most of the night crying, taking walks. I finally fell asleep, which made for late rising, and I neglected my morning ritual. After doing errands, I remain tired. Always busy but not accomplishing anything. While visiting Laura, I made lists of things to do when I came back here. They seemed perfectly doable there, but now I'm here, everything is overwhelming.

March 7

I listened to a radio program discussing the stages of grief: denial, blaming God, blaming the other person, blaming oneself, guilt, grief over never seeing the other person again. If we get caught in an anger stage, we can get clinically depressed. Symptoms of unforgiveness are anger, depression, and self-hate. Please, God, I do not want to stay stuck.

March 8

I wake at 3:45 a.m. Gene, I wake with the knowledge, the gut-level knowing, that chemo destroyed the end of our life together. We had a precious bond for four months, from his diagnosis until July, when the upsetting, confusing behaviors that were the result of chemo destroyed it. Gene, you told me I couldn't understand because I had never gone through it myself. You were right. I kept saying you had a choice by the power of the Holy Spirit. I was wrong. The chemo destroyed your mind and your spirit along with your body. I hate it. Barbaric, damnable treatment. Forgive me, sweetheart, for my lack of understanding, compassion, and patience. The things that upset me, I realize now, weren't you. It was the chemo.

> I can't settle down.
> Can't read.
> Can't write.

I remember feeling betrayed by the medical community when, during your daylong Taxol treatments, I read the literature lying around the office and learned that during testing, a new drug is deemed "successful," if, for example, a patient with a prognosis of six months lives nine. Your prognosis was five months, and you lived nine. Your treatment will go down in the annals of medical history as a success. I have very different criteria! I miss you terribly.

March 9

Dear God, help me remember Emmet Fox today, "Bless a thing, and it will bless you. If you bless a situation, it will have no power to hurt you." I find myself repeating, "Goddamn the devil, damn the chemo, damn the pain of this moment. Please enable me, oh, God, to bless this gray, rainy, windy day."

March 20

I never before spent so much time considering our eternal life. "I believe in the resurrection of the body," the confession we make in the Apostle and Nicene creeds. Christianity teaches bodily resurrection, and I have to confess that I find the idea mind-boggling. In fact, I don't even know how I could possibly believe it. This was all brought home to me when Jeanne and Laura were here in December and Gene mentally and physically revived, causing Laura to say, "Dad, I came planning to write your eulogy, and you are so much better."

I knew then, when I considered his wasted body, that as much as I believe in God's healing power, it was beyond my faith or comprehension that God could raise him up and restore his body. If I couldn't believe it then, then how much greater is my crisis of faith when the undertaker removed Gene's body, familiar and recognizable, and brought me back a few days later a container less than twelve by eight inches I believe in the resurrection of the body?

When you leave your mother and father and cleave unto your spouse, you become one body. One body? That's why these eternal life questions are so powerful now. Does that mean a part of me has died? Does that mean a part of Gene is alive in me?

The other day, I had an appointment to have my 1997 income tax prepared. I thought it would be awfully painful going back over the entire year. It turned out not so. The preparer, Ed Weatherby, was such a kind, compassionate man.

I shall go back to Laura's in a day or two.

March 27

I'm at Laura's, been here for a week. When I tried to return to Virginia yesterday, I got so overcome with grief as I headed south I turned around and went back north at least three times. To an observer, I'm sure I looked like a crazy woman. I felt like a crazy woman. Not until later did it become clear to me why I had to stay one more night.

I'm awake at three o'clock in the morning, starving. I fix a cheese sandwich and cocoa and settle down to read more of John Sandford's book on dreams. Return to sleep around four thirty. *I have an hour and a half till six, the right amount of time to have a dream. God, please speak to me.* A little while later, Laura bursts into my room, crying hysterically. She has had a vivid dream. Since I always have paper and pencil at hand, ready to record dreams, I calmly record her emotional rendition. She is overwhelmed by seeing, smelling, feeling her dad.

The dream—Laura is in her kitchen, and I'm in her living room. Movement catches her eye through the window, and she sees her father. He's on her deck. He's in his work clothes and has come to get a pipe fitting. Looking straight at her, he puts his finger to his lips, motioning silence, so no one else can see him. She calls me, and I come to the window, while she goes outside onto her deck to be with him. He then raises his arms and ascends as a large beautiful white bird and flies high in the sky. He circles around and comes back, lands on her shoulder, and wraps her in his wings. He feels like him even though he is a bird. He then changes to human form saying, "Anytime you need me, just call and I'll be here." He then flies away. As he circles in the air, she has an errant thought, *I hope nobody shoots him.* He comes back and enfolds her in his wings again. She asks him if he had seen his mother, her Nana. He says he has, but she

---

---

can't change form like he can, which he doesn't do often because it hurts his back when he lands. He says with a laugh.

She keeps repeating over and over that she can't get over what it felt like when he enfolded her in his wings.

Now I know why I couldn't return to Virginia. I needed to be here to share this rich dream, to be with her and to record it. There is a dream theory that contends that dreams of the deceased signal a transformation of the mourning process. I hope this is true in our case.

Around noon I leave for Virginia.

During those early weeks of March, as I spent days going back and forth between Virginia and New Jersey, Laura gave me several massages. Those sessions were a blessing. Touching and being touched reaffirmed my life and my existence as a living, breathing human being. It brought healing in a deeper way as I became even more aware of my feelings. Alexander Lowen says in *Betrayal of the Body*, "People are afraid to feel their bodies. On some level they are aware that the body is a repository of their repressed feelings, and while they want to know about them, they are loath to encounter them in the flesh." When feelings came to the surface as a result of a treatment with Laura, I was able to acknowledge and release them.

March 29

I spend the morning planting an early garden . . . kale, spinach, chard, arugula, and fennel. In the afternoon, I walk on the beach. I have meeting with the owner of an antique shop about working weekends while she's away for a month.

March 30

I feel very sad even though I am blessed with beautiful weather and a lawn mower that starts on the first tug of the cord after sitting all winter. I'm struggling with hurt and anger over Jeanne Marie and the fact that when she left in a rush in January, she left her cat with me temporarily because her new husband is allergic. I could not keep my cat and her cat, Jesse, in the same house as they hate one another, so I have kept him in the trailer. But after being a house cat and depending on human companionship, he is suffering. When the Jesse problem is solved, I feel I will no longer need her cooperation and, hopefully, will be as far away from these negative emotions as the 2,400 miles I am away from her physically.

April

I spend my days crying while gardening, crying while mulching with pine shats, crying while walking the beach. As Holy Week begins, I experience new insights and revelations. I have a myriad of dreams, which inspire me with a desire to decipher their meaning, and my dreamwork begins in earnest. Although emotionally fragile, I'm happy with the understanding that comes to me about Gene, my family, and myself. These insights are sparked by the reading I am doing in *Dreams and Healing,* by John Sanford, an Episcopal priest and Jungian therapist. He says the unconscious is revealed in dreams. I have dreams every night and record them. At first I find no meaning in them, so I read other books on dreamwork:

Symbols of Transformation in Dreams and *The Hero's Journey in Dreams* by Jean and Wallace Clift, therapists—she's also an Episcopal priest.

At a Journal Workshop and *The Practice of Process Meditation* by Ira Progoff, psychotherapist.

The Cloud of Unknowing, a late fourteenth-century anonymous work of Christian mysticism.

The Anima, a Book about the Soul, by Tertullian, one of the church fathers. He says, "The dream is the most usual way God reveals himself to man."

The Pregnant Virgin, by Marion Woodman, Jungian analyst, inspired me with this: "A new widow is in a Sacred Space. She is in an altered state of consciousness. Her ego is weakened and she is in direct contact with the unconscious, vulnerable to transpersonal energy that can change her life."

Dreams and Spiritual Growth: A Judeo-Christian Way of Dreamwork, by Louis Savary, contends that, "Dreams are viewed as an intervention from God. They are gifts of consciousness; a possibility for insight, plus the energy to act on the insight."

Living alone provides me with the time and solitude to recall, record, and meditate on these dreams. I enter into a contemplative season of my life. *The Cloud of Unknowing* states that "the contemplative life can be experienced, not from withdrawing physically from the world, but by the withdrawal of psychological attachments from individuals, objects, and relationships. The normal tendency of consciousness is to move outward to sensory contacts, social feelings, and relationships. This results in a dissipation of psychic energy. The first requirement is to call a halt to this by disciplined attention to the mind. A contemplative is one who aims to control his or her thoughts and feelings through special disciplines in order to become capable of a closer relationship with God." Since my desire had always been to have a close relationship with God, to know him better, I realize I have been blessed to have had all my attachments torn from me, and to live on an island, on the water, that inspires and supports the spiritual dimension of life.

Returning to my journal . . .

April 5

Palm Sunday. The scripture for the day, "These present afflictions are nothing compared to the glory set before us." Is that the purpose of this period of my life? I hadn't made having a career, supporting myself, the purpose of my life. Although that was all Gene and my parents did, it never resonated with me.

The purpose of my life? The glory set before me? Wow.

I worked all day yesterday in the antique shop. It was painful coming home afterward, but being at the shop was good therapy for me. When Gene was with me, I loved coming home to an empty house, knowing I would have a few minutes of undistracted time. Now the empty house is a sorrow. Dear God, may I learn to love the moment because every moment, no matter how many years that moment is, passes away.

Bless the moment . . . Have gratitude in the moment . . . Live the moment, for every moment passes away . . . Earth itself shall pass away . . . Nothing is forever . . . Bless the moment.

April 7

Today I am able to pray for Jeanne Marie without hurt or anger. Realizing how adversity either destroys a relationship or makes it stronger, I ponder her exit from our life. I recall when my parents divorced the day Gene and I married. I exited from theirs. I had nothing to give. I was too needy myself. At the time, I was unaware of my need, and I certainly wasn't aware of theirs. All I knew was the relationship was tense and uncomfortable, and I preferred to not be with them. Jeanne has nothing to give, so how can I stay angry? To remain angry would be like hating myself.

Grant me the grace, oh, God, to receive her and mend this. I don't want to be like my father was in the early 1970s when I tried to mend my relationship with him. He destroyed any future closeness by telling me he was glad I finally realized it was all my fault. It was clear then that my mother could never have returned to him if she had second thoughts after their divorce. She would have always been the guilty one.

April 8

I am more grateful for Laura Beth than words can say. She has called me every morning since Gene died just to say, "Good morning, I love you." She is the one person who touches my soul, without whom I would just as soon die, but I don't want her to be burdened by this fact.

Will and Mary came down on Monday. It's nice to have neighbors next door for a while. I had more company on Tuesday, and today Emily invited me to lunch. Nice as they all are, I'm getting a bit people "overdone," and I'm in need of quiet time.

Woke up with a headache and lots of crying, some of it over Jeanne and how she has handled (or not handled) this cat thing. I am convinced now that she doesn't want Jesse. Feeling the way I do about my cat, her behavior is beyond my comprehension, but I must accept what is an obvious truth. Today I will talk to Emily. She's lived on the Shore a long time, is the pastor of a Methodist church, and knows a lot of people. I'll also talk to Barbara Clifford at my church. She lives on a large farm. Maybe between them we can solve the Jessie problem.

April 9

From *Dreams and Healing*, "When we are straying from the path, God becomes our adversary in a broken relationship. Our egocentricity must be countered in this way if we are not to miss the mark." I thank you, God, I have been hurt by Jeanne. By doing so, I am becoming healed. If she had remained in New Jersey, I'm sure I would have made my grandchildren the focus of my life, the purpose of my life. When Gene told me last April that God has a purpose for my life and I need to find out what it is and do it, he confirmed what I know is true. I do not yet know the purpose. But I do know what the purpose is not. It is not to be a grandmother! This realization gets me laughing, and I have no idea why. I'm full of joy bubbles. Strange reaction, because I always wanted to be a grandmother. My Gram was the emotional rock of my life. I loved her, and I wanted to be like her. Now I'm laughing because what I thought I always wanted is never going to be. *Lead me, Lord. Thou will show me the path of life.*

April 10

Good news. Barbara Clifford will take Jessie, the cat, to her farm. She has sheep, goats, cats, dogs, and loves animals. She will love him and give him a good home.

April 11

Holy Saturday. "Who has commanded and it came to pass, unless the Lord hath ordained it? Is it from the mouth of the most high that good and evil come?" (Lamentations 3:37). I accept that nothing happens unless God wills it! Things may not turn out as I want, but

I'm not running the show. Acceptance is the key. God will take all my pain and sorrow and transform them into life.

April 14

My scripture reading for today: "As a father cares for his children, so does the Lord care for those who fear him. He knows what we are made of. He remembers we are dust," (Psalm 103:13–14). This is a very sobering thought in light of the fact that last evening, I had a three-year-old-type temper tantrum. I was cleaning out the closet underneath the stairs and found the box of Gene Fusco Plumbing work order tablets. I threw them across the room. I threw other things and yelled at God, "You could have made it all work out differently. You could have healed Gene. You could have prevented the whole sordid ordeal. Why didn't you? Why didn't you?" I cried and I cried and I cried. I was a child—a mass of emotion, a child with no vision of the larger picture, the larger purpose, or of eternity. I was a child very angry with her daddy. I was a child in the grip of a seemingly unloving, uncaring parent. Powerless!

God! God, you know I regret my immature behavior. You know I can't promise you that I won't do it again. God, I appreciate that you know what I'm made of, that your mercy is great, that you remove my sins from me, that you crown me with mercy and loving kindness. God, I praise you that I am not ashamed at all in your presence, not belittled nor chastised nor humiliated. The crown fits perfectly. I love you, Abba Father.

I dreamed last night with little recall. Tried to write notes in my half-sleep state. Intending to write "dead patches of lawn," I instead wrote "dead patches of law," which I think might be meaningful. I also remember the color purple, which can denote the Seventh Chakra, healing center, heavenly heart, offering opportunities for wisdom, integration and mastery.

April 16

Today Laura and Bob her husband are coming. Also, I've made arrangements to take Jessie, the cat, to Barbara Clifford. It is 4:30

a.m., and the moon is so full the birds are singing. They think it's dawn. The laughing gulls arrived on March 28 between two and four in the afternoon, and the rookery is making a racket. It is so beautiful here; where else could I live? It is so painful here; how can I live? The pain over the loss of my entire adult life is crushing. This end may well be a beginning, but a beginning of what?

Psalm 146, "I will praise the Lord as long as I live. I will sing praises to my God while I have my being, put not your trust in any child of the earth, for there is no help in them."

Please engrave that on my soul, oh, God. *Simple Abundance* says we swallow life to keep it manageable. After several evenings of wine, I know it isn't a glass of wine I want; it's inner peace and deeper connection. Carl Jung says alcoholism is a sacred disease, a spiritual disease. Are not drinks called "spirits"? I need to learn to go inside and ask my soul what I need.

"How can I care for you at this moment?"

April 20

I had asked God to reveal himself to me before I went to sleep last night. When I wake emotional from a dream and go downstairs, Laura says my eyes look like I lost something and cannot find it. I told her I guess I lost my place in the world, my function in the world, my purpose in the world. I dawns on me I have to tell everyone that I am Gene's wife. When I meet a former plumbing customer in town, I always have to tell them I am Gene's wife. I have to reveal my identity. I just can't remain a stranger to them. Last week I had a fleeting thought (which I ignored): *Why do you have to tell everybody who you are?* I need to know I am other than Gene's wife! I am more than Gene's wife! That was my persona for thirty-five years—my persona, not my*self,* not *me.* After talking with Laura a few minutes, I go back to my room to record my dream.

The dream . . . I'm dressed in a white cotton no-frills bra, like in the old Maidenform ads. Later I pull on a man-tailored tweed blazer. I am not uncomfortable or embarrassed or inappropriate in my bra and blazer. (All the dream books say that your clothing signifies your persona.) Insight! I am a woman of the 1950s dressing myself in a man's role—that is, the head of the household, the decision-maker, the motivator, the boss. I'm getting excited as I write. If men only knew what power lay in that tweed jacket! I can now be it all! Today, Monday, the jacket is oversized but rightly appropriate to my perception. I may appear strange to others in my Maidenform and tweed, but I am very happy.

Well, I'm very happy until I go back downstairs to find that Laura's husband, Bob, is taking her home immediately! I am very disappointed. I had looked forward to spending the morning with her. I am upset. She is upset. She's upset with herself because she didn't want to come here in the first place at this time. She has a big test tomorrow and knew she wouldn't study here. Now, leaving abruptly, she has my disappointment to deal with. She's caught between pleasing Bob and pleasing me. I am angry at Bob for whisking her away, especially in light of the fact he's been dependable and supportive since Gene died. Pain. Crying. A big emotional fray. End result? I must let Laura go. I will not have her torn between Bob and me, and so they leave. I have now lost everyone. I give her to you, God. I give her to freedom, growth, maturity, and wholeness. She owes me nothing. It is possible we may have no future together. Every person I have loved with my whole heart is now gone. Oh, God, you run a tough school. Did you not say anyone who loves anything more than me is not fit for the kingdom of God. Leave all and follow. It isn't like I wasn't warned, right?

Thank you, God, for the dream. It seems to be making all of this bearable.

April 21

Dream . . . I am sitting at a dining or kitchen table telling the wife of a young man about my new freedom. I recount my sorrow at losing Gene but end with the freedom of yesterday's insights of the Madenform Tweed Jacket dream.

I wake feeling upbeat, strong, peaceful, and optimistic, with warmth and energy spreading upward from my chest. Thank you, my God! The coffee is excellent, thank you. The sun is bright, thank you. The birds are praising you with gusto!

In the afternoon, I power wash the front deck and mow the lawn. It looks good. Hope Gene can see it. I go and sit on the dock to watch the sunset. Have a beer with Gene. Talk to him. Talk to God. Cry and cry. The water is so beautiful tonight. I love it here and do not want to be in any other place.

April 22

Barbara Clifford called to say Jessie the cat is doing very well. He's definitely a "people cat," and he loves her grandchildren. He's working his way up and will soon be "top dog" in the house! I am very happy that he is okay.

April 29

In *The Cloud of Unknowing*, chapter 23, I read that if we are called to the contemplative life, God will defend us, care for us, stir other men in spirit to give us the things that are necessary for us in this life—food, clothing, etc. He will send us an abundance of necessities or sufficient strength to bear our need. I believe this applies to me, especially when a neighbor stops by in the afternoon and tells me he will keep me supplied with fish. I also had some building supplies I wanted carted away and told the man he could keep the money when he sold them. He refused. I repeated the offer. He refused again. So I gratefully thanked him and accepted the profit.

May

May 5

My friend thinks I'm wonderful, an exotic treasure, and I am concerned about the psychological phenomenon, transference, because I recognize that I am very vulnerable. Since Gene died, there is no one to whom I am most valuable. I have lost all sense of belonging, of family, of a loving relationship, and of interaction. At times I feel total rejection, and I am angry about it. I'm again shedding tears over Gene, which I haven't done in several days.

May 7

I wake after a sound night's sleep to early-morning fog breaking up. I have taken to sleeping in the front bedroom and am enjoying this time of year, as one by one the fishing boats go out to sea. They continue to pleasure me after all these years of living here.

Thank you, God. You continue to bless my soul with the greatness of your love toward me. I realize in order to receive the gift of your treasuring me, I need both hands to hold the gift. If I reach out to receive the gift from another, I will drop yours. And yours is the only one big enough to satisfy my soul, my longings, my desires. Thank you.

May 17

Dream . . . Much activity, many people. Gene and I are staying in a small one-room building. Our Chrysler van is parked nearby. Gene drives away in the van. Floods come. The van is sinking. I go to get him, but water is everywhere. I finally find a man who tells me Gene had left for higher ground a long time ago. Why, oh, why, didn't he take me with him? Why didn't he come and get me? Rescue me?

"It just never occurred to him," the man responded. "He just didn't take his commitment and obligation to you seriously," the man said. I am very upset.

May 21

I'm depressed. Feel as if I can't function. Where is my garment of praise? Where is my beauty? Where is the oil of gladness? I'm frustrated. I'm angry. Why did Gene leave me? I see an eighty-three-year-old neighbor who was close to death a few months ago, out mowing his grass. Gene, I'm really angry at you for leaving me. On top of that, I've had people telling me what I should do, what I could do, what I ought to do. I'm sick of other people telling me what I want!

May 22

Weeping may endure for the night, but joy cometh in the morning. It is a most beautiful, perfect morning and the precious hummingbird just came. I feel completely fulfilled as I sit here on the porch with my six-o'clock coffee. The lawn I mowed yesterday looks lovely. Adding to that loveliness is the fact that I'm not pushing myself to accomplish anything or to perform in any way today. I accept I am free to just be.

June

June 7

My cousin calls to tell me about a friend of hers who lost his wife and has moved to the Eastern Shore. He's interested in meeting me. May she give him my number? "Yes" . . . but I am uneasy and definitely not interested in having a man in my life.

June 14

I had dinner with my cousin's friend. I felt strange, awkward, and am not attracted to him at all. I refuse an invitation for a second "date."

June 26

I've had numerous crying spells over the past week. Crying over Gene's liveliness just six days before he died. Tears and more tears.

June 27

I take a long relaxing bath before I go to bed. I ask Gene to come to me, reassure me, give me a sign. I'm overwhelmed with sadness with each new realization that he is gone. I just can't believe it.

Dream . . . I am in my bed, sleeping on my left side, when Gene comes into the room and takes my right hand in his. The pressure of his hand, his presence, is so real I know he's here in a very strong, comforting way.

I wake and cry and cry because he isn't here. Is this the sign I asked for before I went to sleep?

I trust that it is.

July

July 18

A least once a day this past week, I have cried over Gene, over the loss of his personhood, his life in this world realm, even though I have a greater sense of God's presence and provision for me than ever.

Without you, oh, my God, my friend, I would die.

July 26

I awake to a gentle, soaking rain, the first moisture in two weeks. It is very gray, very damp, like I am. It's Gene's birthday. He would be sixty-one.

July 27

The saltwater cowboys are driving the ponies down the beach to pen them in preparation for the swim on Wednesday. Seeing the ponies and cowboys emerge from the early-morning mist is my favorite part of Pony Penning week. The beach, the ocean, the colorful sunrise and Chincoteague ponies . . . the story of the beginning of my love for this place.

August 1998

Month of My Birthday and Wedding Anniversary

I've been keeping busy. I work part-time at a pottery shop, a gift shop, and an antique shop. I'm doing yard work, creating new flower beds for a friend. I devote a lot of time to church work and counseling. Add to this, meals with friends and daily walks on the beach. Full days. Meaningful days. Yet I enter an extended period of questioning my path, my purpose, my destination, and how I get there. My dreams are of being lost and not knowing how to find my way.

Laura visits for the first time since April. I feel she is the only person in the world I can trust. Recently betrayed by a close friend, I want to go home with her. Of course, I don't go home with her. I refuse to live as a satellite of my daughter's life. I tell myself, "Trust in the Lord only." I question why I'm still vulnerable to being thrown off balance and hurt by betrayal. Though I felt betrayed by Gene when his self-punishing and self-destructive tendencies caused him to withdraw from me, no one now is close enough to me to elicit this hurt. I'm perplexed.

For days I feel hungover, heavyhearted, and sad, without energy or zest for life. The sense of adventure and anticipation of what God would do has turned into the burden of living my life alone.

A friend expresses a desire for me to help her build a house on a lot she owns, but that does not materialize. Laura and Bob talk about leaving New Jersey and buying a farm where I can have a small cottage on the property and help with the animals. That idea does not come to fruition either. I know I can put no trust in human flesh. Does not the scripture say, "Blessed is the man who trusts in God, but cursed is the man who trusts in man"? The arm of flesh will fail you. I can't build a life with Laura and Bob. I can't build a life with my house-building friend. There is no one with whom I can build a life. My heart turns toward Gene and his memory. I can't build a life with him, for sure. I am alone. And those on whom I have pinned my heart are, in many ways, weaker than I. I am alone.

God, why do I need the illusion of not being alone? Why am I looking for something or someone other than you, oh, God?

August has been extremely hot and humid, but on the eleventh, the day before my birthday, rain comes with majestic lightning, and I feel rested for the first time in days. Wonder if my improved feeling is due to my acceptance of the fact that I am alone, or the change in atmospheric pressure.

August 12

Early-morning sweet breezes kiss the wind chimes and the nape of my neck, bringing peace. Bill and Irene Rouse call to sing "Happy Birthday." They invite me to a celebratory lunch at the Snow Hill Inn, a lovely place in Maryland.

In the evening when I return from a walk on the beach, I find a sweet "Happy birthday, I love you," voice mail from Jeanne.

Our wedding anniversary is the twenty-eighth. My emotions are close to the surface. I want some relief from this sadness. As is my lifelong habit, I turn to books. I find ideas I hope will help in Gerald May's *The Awakened Heart—Living beyond Addiction, Will and Spirit, Care of Mind—Care of Spirit, Simply Sane, The Dark Night of the Soul.* I fill my journal with notes from them.

In *Will and Spirit*, May says we get attached to an emotion when we harbor resentment, anger, or unforgiveness. I know I'm attached to terrible sadness and anger about chemo, oncologists, and Gene's physical and emotional condition. I am faced with the strength of my attachment when I pass David on the causeway on my way to the mainland. He owes me $40. I'm angry with him. But it immediately comes to my mind the fact that I owe the oncologist $4000.

Ah, all have sinned and come short of the glory of God. I am guilty. I am very angry with the doctors! Why should I pay them for putting Gene through hell?

My hatred and horror over the situation, and my refusal to forgive, has been my justification for not paying the $4000. This unwillingness to pay has me stuck. I must pay the bill. I don't want to pay it, but If I don't pay, I'll stay stuck. I'll not go forward. God can't lead me, guide me, bless me. God, I'm willing to be made willing.

Compounding my anger is a call from Laura. She's upset about a piece she saw on television about Taxol, the chemo Gene was on. It's been discovered that the solution they put Taxol in caused allergic reactions (killing reactions?), and they have discontinued its use. Patients as guinea pigs, that's all. She tells me she hopes I never pay them. More fuel for my angry fire. "Why, oh, why, do I have to pay?" I wail. Even though I know I must, it is hard—so hard—to do so.

I wish I were dead. My life is too heavy for me to carry. I have no one dependent on me whom I need to keep living for. I feel like Elijah, the prophet, running from Jezebel, believing the lie that I am alone. I remember when I was twenty-seven, lying on my living room floor, crying, "God, if there is a God, let me die."

God came to me in saving grace and gave me a new life. But now what?

What now?

Stuck.

I'm stuck till Hebrews 13:5 comes alive, "Be satisfied with your present circumstances and with what you have, for he, God himself, has said, I will not in any way fail you, nor give you up, nor leave you without support. I will not, I will not, I will not in any degree leave you helpless, nor forsake you, nor let you down, nor relax my hold on you. Assuredly not." God, help me believe this with my whole heart.

I don't sense God's presence. I am very depressed, but somewhere I am assured I'll be okay.

I apply to myself this quote from *Care of Mind—Care of Spirit*: "Spiritual growth is always accompanied by the lessening of attachments. [Oh, boy, have my attachments been ripped away.] This can lead to a mild, low-level sadness that colors a person's overall attitude. It leads to disorientation and feelings of uncertainty that represent a movement towards the 'not-knowing' that accompanies the lessening of attachments."

Gerald May goes on to contrast the differences between the depressed person and one who experiences the dark night of the soul.

(1) Dark night continues to function, especially in helping others on their spiritual journey, unlike depression.
(2) Dark night retains a sense of humor, not cynical or bitter, after psychological responses of fear, anger, etc.
(3) Compassion for others is enhanced in the dark night. Depression results in self-absorption.
(4) Underneath the superficial confusion, the person in the dark night would have it no other way. The depressed wants a radical change due to a deep sense of wrongness.
(5) The dark night does not seem to be pleading for help as a depressed person does.
(6) Most important, one does not feel frustrated, resentful, or annoyed in the presence of a dark night soul, as one would in the presence of a depressed person (due to their great internalized anger).

So, Barbara, which are you?

August 28 (our thirty-fifth wedding anniversary)

I think all I ever wanted was to be with Gene. From the moment he asked me to cha-cha the night we met, we had a connection, and all my desire to go to grad school and teach in a university flew out the window. It was love-lust at first sight. I remember we spent every night together dining, dancing, drinking. He introduced me to his parents, and we made plans to marry as soon as possible. Six weeks from meeting to marriage. From that time till the day he died, other men were invisible to me. *I love you. I miss you. I must have been a terrible person, for God to punish me by taking you away.* Intellectually, I know that's not true, but that's how I feel.

Black Monday, August 31

The stock market falls over five hundred points. Gabriela, my grand-daughter, is celebrating her second birthday in Arizona. There's the smell of fall in the air. The still, muggy, winding down of summer has enfolded me in a deep, deep sadness—a weighty heavy cloak, oppressive as the humidity on my skin.

September

September 11

Dream . . . Gene and I are in our van. I'm driving. We're on a beach, lots of sand, lots of water—a bay, not an ocean. He's urinating near a house, spattering lattice. I realize we're trespassing. His hip bones are very sore, and I know he is going to die even though earlier I had assurance that he would be healed.

Awake. This is what I come up with working with the dream: beach is a boundary or threshold. To go further, I need to swim or boat, so new qualities are needed, requiring a test of confidence and daring; urination symbolizes the flow of life through us.

Dear God, if I am parked on the sand with Gene as his life force is being spilled out, please let me release him totally to you and release myself to move on in the direction you would have me to go; to push out into the deep; to look with anticipation to the life you are calling me to live.

September 12

Dream . . . I'm doing a lot of moving, packing, getting rid of. I hear a voice saying, "If you want to be free and travel around, you can't have any more possessions than you can carry."

God, is this an answer to my prayer to release Gene and move on?

September 13

It's Sunday, and after church I go to work in the pottery shop. I feel physically and spiritually burdened. I am glad to meet Veronica from hospice whom I had spoken to on the phone. A pleasant contact, but when I come home to my empty house, I feel just like the day Gene died. I wander aimlessly, try to nap. I'm drowning in grief. How long will this go on?

September 24

Emily and I return from a three-day trip to a retreat center in Connecticut. It's good to be home. So beautiful and peaceful here. Home. Yet just yesterday morning, I felt homeless after we had stayed in a motel in New Jersey ten miles from where I was born and where I had lived for forty-nine years. A motel. I had nowhere else to go. I was a visitor. I was displaced. I belonged to none of it. Pain. Pain of the loss of my life. I belonged to no one, and no one belonged to me. I wanted to go home, but I didn't have a home to go to. It was all so near, yet so far, just like Gene. Drove back to Chincoteague, exhausted and spent. Now, this morning, I'm blessed to feel good to be home. *I do have a home. Thank you, God.* Weeping may endure for the night, but joy comes in the morning.

September 26

Dream . . . boiling eggs for Easter—at least one hundred of them— then I find out I might be expected to boil a thousand. The first batch of eggs I had to peel (doesn't seem to fit the Easter egg theme).

Dreamwork—eggs symbolize new birth, breaking out of one's shell; a hundred and a thousand can symbolize God, spiritual creativity, independence, and unity. I take encouragement from this.

September 27

Dream . . . I'm working out of my position as a single woman, expressing my desire never to marry again. I lock myself in a motel room at Christmas using three locks on the door so no man could come into my life. Three people were trying to convince me that I wouldn't be alive again until I had a sexual relationship and married again. I rejected that totally. There were other scenarios during the night, all with the alone theme. One scenario, I'm alone, not by my own choice. In another, I choose to be alone. I do not want, need, nor desire a man in my life.

Now awake, the meaning seems clear. My sleeping and waking life are in sync. I believe my conscious and subconscious are at one. I do not appear to be double-minded! I am beloved of YHWH. The Lord my Maker is my husband.

I rejoice in the cool, clear, quiet morning and most of all, in the sense of God's wonderful peace, love, and joy.

October

Early in the month, I call the Diocese of Southern Virginia for information about the Ordination Exploration Program. I spend the month thinking and praying about this, while continuing my part-time work in several shops and my church work. The end result is that I do not enter the program. I think it's too long and too expensive. I wonder if even the apostles would qualify.

On the twenty-first, I say, *Happy Birthday Laura, God bless.*

The car needs an inspection sticker, and since I'm considering going to New Jersey in a few days, the garage will probably be all out of stickers when I come back. I can't find my insurance card, for which I have a cancelled check as proof of payment. I begin to realize that a grief-stricken person is very much like a person who's had too much alcohol. They each feel themselves to be perfectly functional and are unaware that they're not. This was also brought home to me during the summer when I neglected for several months to deposit a check from the church collection. I was very surprised when I discovered this because I believed I was doing just fine.

For the past several weeks, I've had recurring dreams containing the number 3 . . . three people in a car with me, three live kittens, three dead kittens, three leaks in the roof, three people representing death, three nights I'm traveling on a train, and on and on. I don't take time to work with them, but I hope they point to something significant. The number 3 is meaningful in religion, mythology, and numerology.

November

I attend a seminar in Easton, Maryland, given by Dennis, Matthew, and Sheila Linn. Their ministry focuses on healing life's painful memories. The most helpful tool I take from the workshop is the following exercise:

Take fifteen minutes at the end of the day, in a quiet, candlelit place to seek God's guidance by the Ignatian method—which is, to ask yourself, "What made me most happy, blessed, or thankful this day (consolation)? What made me least happy, blessed, or thankful (disconsolation)? Intend to do more of the first and less of the second. I decide to practice this.

Several days after the seminar, I go back to Laura's. She gives me a massage, which incorporates a cranial sacral treatment. We spend time watching old family movies and do a lot of crying. Gene, Jeanne, and the children are all gone. It turns out to be therapeutic but painful. Between the massage and the tears, I am left feeling relaxed and have no trouble going to sleep, unlike the previous night when I needed a glass of wine to settle me.

The next morning I clearly hear in a dream, "Thank you, God, for saving my life now and when I was twenty and when I was seven."

I seem to be busy cleaning out a basement and garage, discarding and sorting. Once fully awake, I feel good, relaxed, and comfortable in my body. All pains I'd suffered for over a week are gone. Cranial sacral is as subtle as an X-ray. I don't understand how it works, but I feel like a different person. Thank you, Laura.

I returned to Virginia on the nineteenth and back again to New Jersey on the twenty-sixth.

While in New Jersey, I begin to practice another Ignatian prayer I learned at the Linn's seminar:

Pray a "grace," a grace is a narrowly defined request, and then read the Gospel for the day. Spend one third of the time in prayer, one third in reading, and one third journaling. God will speak to you. Keep the grace prayer request for one month. God will not only speak out of the scripture but will speak out of worship services, people, and other books. After several days seeking guidance about what "grace" to ask for, I decide on, "How can I best be a sacrament in this world?" A sacrament is an outward and visible sign of an inward and spiritual grace, and I want to be a human reflecting and revealing the Holy Spirit who dwells in me.

I return home December 4.

December

December 14

Genesis 23:3, "There must be a time of standing up from before the dead and ceasing to mourn." As I ask my grace, how I can best be a sacrament in this world, I hear Matthew 9:1–17 telling me that the former fabric of my life cannot be altered to fit my life now. I have a new and renewed spirit, and I have a new calling, path, purpose. Oh, God, enable me to rejoice in it.

December 16

The answer to my "grace" prayer is to let God be the planner. According to Matthew 10:1–20, God provides the call, the power, and the job description. Verse 9 tells me to trust in God by not having my own worldly resources. Verse 10 promises I will have my needs met. Verse 16 confirms I am sent out. And verse 20 assures me

God speaks in, through, and out of me. *May these promises be actualized in me, dear God.*

Later in the morning, my dearest friend, Iris, brings me a large Fraser Fir wreath so that I can smell Christmas. How kind, thoughtful, and precious of her. I put it in the center of the dining room table like an Advent wreath.

December 18

Grace prayer, how can I be a sacrament in this world, is answered in Matt 11:1–30.

I ask you to grant me the grace to take your yoke upon me and learn of you. Jesus, you are gentle, not harsh; humble, not proud. You give rest, not disquiet; relief, not pressure; ease, not difficulty; refreshment, not starvation or need; blessed quiet, not turmoil or dismay. Dear Lord, grant me the grace to receive what you give and then to give away to others what you have given me.

December 19

Answer to grace prayer today, Psalm 9:1 and 2: "I will praise you, O Lord, with my whole heart; I will tell of all your marvelous works; I will be glad and rejoice in you; I will sing praise to your name, O Most High."

December 21

Awake at 5:00 a.m. I go out on the side deck to see the stars, but there is too much artificial light to see more than the few most prominent. I meditate on the stars, a large part of God's creation. They can't be seen without darkness. The deeper the darkness, the more of them a person can see. For stargazing one has to stay in the dark long enough for the eyes to adjust. I believe the same holds true for all of God's truths that can be apprehended only in darkness—the darkness of soul despair, suffering, and loss. We dare to enter and to remain in the dark only because we know God loves us and because the darkness can never put out the light.

God, grant that I resist the temptation to lighten my life artificially, thereby missing an opportunity to know you more broadly, deeply, intimately than ever before.

When I'm ready to embrace the darkness, I encounter Ranier Maria Rilke's *Duino Elegies—from the Tenth Elegy:*

> Someday emerging at last from the violent insight,
> let me sing out jubilation and praise to assenting
> angels.
> Let not even one of the clearly-struck hammers
> of my heart
> fail to sound because of a slack, a doubtful, or a
> broken string.
> Let my joyfully streaming face make me more
> radiant;
> let my hidden weeping arise and blossom.
> How dear you will be to me then, you nights of
> anguish.
> Why didn't I kneel more deeply to accept you,
> inconsolable sisters, and surrendering, lose myself
> in your loosened hair.
> How we squander our hours of pain.
> How we gaze beyond them into the bitter dura-
> tion to see if they have an end.

Though reason fails, one thing is sure, my heart overflows with incomprehensible, unexplainable love for you.

December 23

No dreams for several days. I wake at 3:00 a.m. and thank God for delicious coffee. This desire to "embrace my anguish and lose myself in her loosened hair" is followed by much sorrow. I wonder if I shall ever be healed. It seems as if God, by divine fiat took away my entire family. In the past, when Gene was "not there for me," as we say, I could talk with Jeanne and Laura and find pleasure, joy, and love.

Who but God could arrange for all of them to leave me? If this is training in the kingdom, so be it. But I have some questions that have bubbled up from time to time that I need you, o God, to put to rest for me. (1) Have I failed so miserably as a mother or friend or human being that Jeanne would walk out, or run away, at such a critical time in our lives and then basically disappear with an occasional bimonthly phone call? Forgive me, God, but there are moments I take her behavior very personally. (2) Did I put my cat down unnecessarily? If I had been in better shape, could I have had the strength to pray, wait, and nurse him? I believed then and I still see it now, that he was in pain, scared, and unable to keep down even water. But his spirit, his precious, wonderful spirit, reached out to me to the very end. He trusted me. I was like god to him, and I failed him by not being there with my hands on him till his last breath. After Gene's death weeks before, I couldn't take any more. I am so sorry. (3) Am I so hard-hearted, so stubborn, so rebellious, so bad, that you needed to punish me this way, like a child who is not only spanked but beaten? Like a victim of rage who is not shot once but numerous times? Have you found such displeasure in me that you needed to put me through the fire like this? And to what end? As a refinement? Or as a down payment on hell? Oh, God, I seek to grab and deny these questions because of what I know, believe, and trust, based on my salvation experience and my life with you. But I cannot discount them because someone somewhere inside of me is thinking these thoughts and feeling this way. And maybe *feel* is the key word here, because for a child, before intellectualization, comes feeling. We are born into this world under law. We learn law early. We cry too long; we make Mommy mad. We reach out to grab the pretty crystal and get a stern rebuke. We behave, and nobody in our world gets mad. We're good, we get candy. We're bad, we get bed with no supper. Justice. Fairness. Law. It must be part of our DNA. We continue to confirm this fair, just law into adulthood. We are justified in doing to them because they have done to us. An eye for an eye. We expect justice and fairness. We yearn for it. We work very hard at keeping on the right side of the scale. Until one day, grace, God's unearned, unmerited favor, comes and turns our world upside down.

December 24

After days of mild weather, ice began accumulating last evening, and I could see car lights backed up on the causeway due to two accidents. Everything is coated with a thick layer of ice this morning. The ice is thick on the utility wires. I thank you, God, for heat, light, and coffee.

I read Rilke, "What they want from me is that I gently remove the appearance of injustice about their death, which, at times, slightly hinders their souls from proceeding onward."

Oh, God, grant me the grace to release Gene from my desire for justice and understanding.

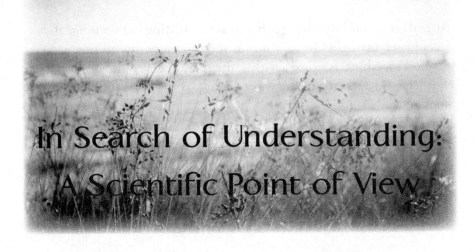

In Search of Understanding: A Scientific Point of View

In the twelfth month of my emotional roller coaster, feeling at times a bit crazy, I come upon a quote of Freud's description of a grieving person:

"A grieving person is insane, albeit a socially acceptable insanity. Each single one of the memories and expectations in which the libido is bound is brought up and hypercathected (extreme emotionalism) and detachment of the libido is accomplished in respect of it. It is remarkable that this painful unpleasure is taken as a matter of course by us."

In an attempt to deal with my hypercathected, my extreme emotional state, I consider Christian mystic, Meister Eckhart:

"If something is, it is God's will. If you truly enjoyed God's will, you would feel the same no matter what happened to you."

Clearly, I am not "enjoying God's will," at least not to that degree. I have railed against the wrongness of Gene's death so many times since his diagnosis, especially in light of my strong faith in the healing power of God.

On the other hand, I am a far cry from Roger Rosenblatt, who—on the sudden death of his thirty-six-year-old daughter Amy—said, "In a way believing in God made Amy's death more, not less, comprehensible, since the God I believe in is not beneficent. He doesn't care. A friend was visiting Jerusalem when he got the news about Amy. He kicked the Wailing Wall and said, 'Fuck you, God.' My sentiments exactly."

I am fortunate to come upon *Blueprint for Immortality*, by Harold Saxton Burr, from which I take copious notes. He was a professor of anatomy at Yale University, who had done experiments in the electrical fields that underlie all life. The main points of his book that I found enlightening and extremely helpful were the following:

(A) Every living system possesses an electrical field of great complexity, which can be measured with considerable accuracy, and all life is connected by these electrical fields. When measurements were taken of trees, air, and earth, they all exhibited changes in their fields at approximately the same time. A change in one was accompanied by a change in the others being measured. They seem to be on the same wavelength, as we commonly say. The moon had previously been believed to be the cause of these changes. Now we know that the moon and all living systems respond to some more Primary Characteristic of the Cosmos.

(B) The state of the mind is reflected in the state of the field. For example, an emotion of grief recalled under hypnosis caused a fourteen-millivolt rise for two and a half minutes. It appears that an idea is just as valid a stimulus as a kick in the teeth. The mind of man does not exist in time, does not occupy space, and involves no energy transformation, as far as anyone knows. The nervous system, through which the mind works, does exist in time, does occupy space, and does require energy transformation. It is a mystery how a nonmaterial attribute, such as mind, is able to actually influence the organic nervous system, but it does.

(C) Electricity is the way nature behaves. This orderly, measurable, patterned phenomena is an essential characteristic of the universe. In the last analysis, the universe is a unit. All of its parts are related to the wholeness of the universe, and there is some interrelationship between the wholeness and its individual components. This can be proven by measuring the electrical fields which exist, which Dr. Burr named L-fields (Life fields).

(D) L-fields are links in a "chain of authority," starting with the simplest forms, running upward through all life on this planet, to men, through space, outward and upward to an ultimate Infinite Authority about which we can only speculate. These fields of life override the normal laws of chemistry and physics. They compel atoms and molecules to assume stable arrangements, which break down to simpler compounds after the death of the form.

(E) We exist by virtue of inexorable laws in a highly organized universe of law and order. The universe has one Designer. It is a Uni (unit set up and maintained by its electrical field). This all-embracing field is the creation and instrument of the Designer. The primary value of the field concept is that it gives meaning for the universe to us, because design and organization imply not only direction but purpose. It supports religions' one God because it eliminates the need for two sets of laws, one material and one spiritual. There is one Designer and one overall field to which all humanity is subject.

(F) We know so little that we still have to think of good and evil as opposites. The only solid definition of good is something that is valid or demonstrably true, something in harmony with known natural laws. The Law of Gravity is true and right. We do not blame it and call it evil if a man defies it and meets his death falling off a cliff. We can be assured that what we call "good" and "evil" are an inherent part of the design of the Universe because there can be *nothing outside that design.*

In my journal in December of 1998, I underline, "Nothing outside that design". My life is part of the oneness of the Universe. Gene's death is part of the oneness of the Universe. Dr. Burr's Designer, Infinite Authority, Primary Characteristic of science was my God of religion. Has not it been said in Isaiah 45:7–8, "I am the Lord, there is no other, there is no God besides me," "I form the light, and create darkness, I make weal and create woe; I the Lord do all these things."

In the face of this Unity, this Mystery, this Ultimate Authority, I joined Meister Eckhart and a multitude of saints and mystics throughout the ages and profess that though I do not understand, I do accept by faith that God works all things together for my good (Romans 8:28).

Footnotes

- *Making Toast: A Family Story,* Roger Rosenblatt, 2010
- *Blueprint For Immortality: The Electric Patterns of Life,* Harold Saxton Burr, 1978

Addendum

Since Harold Saxton Burr (4/16/1889–2/17/1973) experimented in the early to midtwentieth century, others have made much progress building on the foundation he laid. Just two of the many follow:

The Body Electric: Electromagnetism and the Foundation of Life, published 1985 by Robert O. Becker (5/31/1923–5/14/2008), an orthopedic surgeon and researcher in electrophysiology and electro-medicine. He worked mainly as professor at Upstate Medical Center SUNY, Syracuse, and as director of Orthopedic Surgery at the VA Hospital in Syracuse.

Dr. Candace Pert on a PBS special, *Healing and the Mind* with Bill Moyers, responded to his statement, "Oh, what you are talking about is mind *over* matter," with "No, I'm talking about mind *in* matter."

Candace Beebe Pert, PhD (6/26/1946–9/12/2013), was a neuroscientist and pharmacologist who discovered the Opiate Receptor, the cellular binding site for endorphins in the brain. She is the author of *Molecules of Emotion: The Science Between Mind-Body Medicine—1999; Everything You Need to Know to feel Go(o)d —2006.*

This Is My First
Christmas without You

December 25, 4:00 a.m.

This is my first Christmas without you. Unexplored territory. Thick ice coats the world. Warm inside, I give thanks for good coffee and no loss of electricity. The Christmas Eve service at church was canceled, and sections of the mainland are without power.

This morning I am up early like a kid. Though I'm not receiving a gift, I must create a gift, a gift of Christmas past, of memories, of blessings, and then wrap that gift as the treasure that it is and give it away to the only One who can receive it.

Our first Christmas, we were living with my father while we were building our house on McKnight Avenue in Jamesburg on a lot formerly your father's garden. Situated between your parents and your older brother, I called it *Relative Row*. Always the frustrated architect, I drew up the blueprints, and we easily managed to qualify for a construction loan. You and your friends in construction laid the foundation, did the framing and the roof. I helped lay hardwood floors, put in insulation, and painted. My mother and I hung wallpaper. It was difficult living with my father during this time because he was hurt and angry over my mother's departure.

You took me to Christmas Eve service at Saint James Roman Catholic Church, which was foreign to this Presbyterian. Latin, sung mass, and incense created an atmosphere that caused me to look at you standing to my right and ask, *Who is this person? Who is this stranger from another world?*

We went to your parents' house for a big meal afterward. I don't remember any other festivities. I only remember that I was madly in love with you.

Who are you? was to become an oft repeated question in my mind throughout our years together.

Our second Christmas, we had a new home and a new baby. In addition to creating our darling Cape Cod house, our love-lust at first sight had produced a child. You often joked about throwing the brush out of the second-story window as you finished painting the nursery while I was in the hospital giving birth to Jeanne Marie. In spite of the new house and baby, this Christmas was disappointing, because you and family had none of the traditions familiar to me, and my family had been dissolved. My beloved Gram dead. My grandfather with a new wife. My parents divorced. And baby Jeanne Marie a little young to be excited about it all.

For many years, I took over cooking and hosting your mom's traditional Christmas Eve dinner following midnight mass. I wanted tradition. I wanted family, and these were happy holidays. A particular close, loving, meaningful one was the Christmas before your nephew, Jan, was killed in Vietnam. It seemed to be a gift of God's grace before the heartbreak that affected your entire family—a heartbreak from which you never recovered.

In 1966, the year Laura Beth was born, you had too much to drink after leaving work at Hercules in Rocky Hill and went on a Christmas Eve shopping spree at Bamberger's. The dress, sweaters, and slacks were a thoughtful gesture for an overweight mother of an infant and a two-year-old. I will never forget Jeanne's big, dark eyes Christmas morning, filled with excitement at the first sight of the colorfully decorated tree and hobby horse waiting for her.

Not long after that, Hercules in Rocky Hill, where you had worked for several years, relocated to West Virginia, and you got a job at the Dupont Photo Processing Plant in Parlin. Burned in my memory is the night you had acid splashed in your eyes during the second shift. You were wearing eye patches, and someone had driven you home. It was after midnight when you sat on the bed in the dark, gently waking me, telling me not to worry or be upset when you turned on the light. You explained what had happened and that you were fine. Oh, how I wanted to protect you! The only thing I couldn't ever protect you from was my sharp tongue. And cancer.

I remember too the Christmas we had four-foot snowdrifts, and my mother stayed with us several days. On Christmas Eve, you and Tony carried the tea cart through the snow from your mother's house where you had hidden it in her attic. I was delighted with the gift. It was a big surprise.

I remember the year your sister Betty came over early in the morning. We were at the kitchen table when she told us we couldn't move out of Jamesburg to Monroe until your father died because it would kill him if we left. At the young age of twenty-seven, I thought she was rude, controlling, manipulative, and had no right to be telling us what to do. But now I see things differently. Betty was probably right. She must have known how tender or vulnerable he was underneath it all. In her shoes, last year I begged Jeanne not to go to Arizona. How stricken you were when she and Nery exploded and divorced. How heart-broken you were because you loved him but hated what he did. You were torn between your desire to protect Jeanne and little Lucas and your identification with Nery's motivation and behavior.

The corner cabinet, another Christmas gift from you, which stands in the living room with me now as I write is a token of your love . . . you paid attention, you listened, you heard what I wanted.

8:00 a.m.

The rising sun has revealed sparkling diamond-encased trees, marsh grasses, and water. I have been set down in the midst of a crystal palace. A queen couldn't live in a more beautiful castle. Thank you, God, for a glorious morning! I trust, sweet Gene, that the visions that you are privileged to behold far surpass this earthly beauty. I say, sweet Gene, because my heart is pressed, squeezed, twisted, with love for you and for all that you are to me. Your very essence has been knotted into my heart, and just as it is difficult to unknot a delicate gold chain, you will eternally be part of me. Large, bulky chains are easy to unknot, and the memories I have touched on today are similar to those. But the minute chains, formed of unremembered daily events, remain embedded forever in my body and soul. I know I will, from time to time, return to this Christmas package with a few more large links, but for now, oh, my God, I give these twisted piles of precious gold to you for your safekeeping, for only you know what to do with them. If I try to hold on to them, they will crush my broken heart and destroy me. But in your hand, they can be made into a priceless, exquisite ornament that can adorn me according to your will.

> If you keep looking back, you can't see where you
> are going.
> I am no longer wife
> I am no longer mother
> I am no longer grandmother
> Where am I going dressed in the ornaments of God?

The Twelve Days of Christmas

Nearing the first year anniversary of Gene's passing, I expect to feel better. Although I've had many encouraging encounters with God and have enjoyed sporadic happiness, I am not yet out of the woods. Years later, I read that often things get worse around the one-year anniversary because one is now realizing the hard truth that this is the way life will be from now on. In wandering the wilderness of grief, one year is nothing at all. I find myself saying over and over that the New Year is almost here, and I want God to give me resolution for this past one. I want resolution in all meanings of the word—*resolution*, as in a settled, determined solution. I'm seeking for things to be resolved, loosened, broken up, transformed, and assured. Or as in *Webster's* definition of a musical resolution, "the progression of a dissonant tone of a chord to the tone of another pitch so as to produce a consonant tone." Yes, consonance, harmony, that's what I'm seeking.

The day after Christmas, I wake with a dream image:

There are two singers—an older male, a famous singer, off-key, flat. He's doing a duet with a young, unknown woman with clear, perfect pitch, who is extremely musically gifted. *Hummmm . . . might this be the musical resolution I am looking for?* I think in my half dream state.

Fully awake now, I'm reading Stephen Mitchell, and I want his translation of Psalm 147 to minister to my soul . . .

How sweet to sing praises to you.
Unnameable God,
and to thank you for all your blessings.
You build what has been ruined
and recreate what was lost.
You heal the brokenhearted;
you are medicine for their wounds.

Leaving Mitchell, I return to Meister Eckhart, German mystic, born in 1260, who counsels:

You might ask, "How can I know if something is God's will?" My answer is, if it were not God's will, it wouldn't exist, even for an instant; so if something happens, it must be his will. If you truly enjoyed God, you would feel the same, no matter what happened to you."

This is a hard saying, God. How can I accept this? How is it possible to believe that you rule over all the world? That you send your angels to do your bidding. That your will is always done. I'm willing to believe it. I know I must choose my life as it is. It is a gift from you. Since you rule over all, how much more perfect is your rule over your own children? My marriage has been dissolved. I am alone. I accept it as your gift to me. I choose to accept the gift. I choose it. I am sorry about Gene, but to entertain any idea that your will was not done is nothing but rebellion.

I choose the gift.
I choose widowhood.
I choose my life as it is.
Oh, God, grant me the grace to delight in it.

In addition to reading Mitchell and Eckhart, I begin a book of daily meditations by Sister Francis Clare, *Glory to Glory*. I take this word from her as God's word to me today:

The Lord is waiting to show you favor,
He rises to pity you . . .
He will be gracious to you when you cry out,
as soon as He hears He will answer you.

No longer will your Teacher hide himself,
but with your own eyes you shall see your teacher.
While from behind, a voice shall sound in your ears:
"This is the way; walk in it, when you would turn
to the right or the left." (Isaiah 30:18)

Inspired by Sister Francis's translation I begin to sing this in a spontaneous plain song, as the words and notes minister medicine to my soul.

The Second Day of Christmas

Sunday

I wake this morning with a deep sense of peace and joy. God is bringing resolution. I think my subconscious supports my confidence. A series of dreams involving changes of clothing indicate to me that a change in ways of adapting to my life situation is evolving. My old clothes are inadequate to my present situation. I have a new raincoat and wearing raincoats can symbolize the attitudes we use to meet difficult emotions with the release of tears, rain. They often appear in dead spouse dreams. My real life and my dream life—what I like to call, my real life and my reel life—seem to be in sync.

After four days of crying, I go to church, to be told how wonderful I look. No wonder they don't think I'm needy. I guess I give the appearance of having it all together by the time God gets me there. I don't want to give a false impression. I do want to be real with them, but I guess my Sunday reality is resting in God and looking good. At six o'clock, my Methodist pastor friend, Emily, and I do a worship service at the Hermitage—an assisted-living facility in Onancock—and I deliver a message that's based on the insight I had about seeing stars only in the dark. Afterward, I'm told my voice has "life" in it. I'm grateful to God, thrilled that my words have life and are food for people. Thank you, God, thank you.

I began Christmas morning, saying that I was receiving no gift. At that moment it was true to the best of my knowledge.

On the first day of Christmas, I realized I have a gift I intend to receive with my whole heart. That gift being my life. That gift being widowhood. That gift being the graciousness of the Lord. That gift being the knowing that God is good, God is good all the time.

New Year's Day, 1999

At 4:00 a.m. on this anniversary day, memory comes knocking at the door, calling my name, carting a briefcase of recollections, feelings, and images. My second-story bedroom in the charming old waterman's cottage on South Main Street overlooking Chincoteague Bay provides a grand view of the moonlight shimmering on the water in the early-morning darkness. My spirits are lifted as usual by the glorious sight. I bless the crews heading for open water on brightly lit fishing boats. I remember a young man who had gone down on one of those ships. Sole survivor, he is wracked by post-traumatic stress so severe that his young wife was driven to say, "You know, dying is not always the worst thing that can happen."

After I go downstairs and coffee is brewed, I sit in the living room, journal in hand, and replay in my mind every second of the morning Gene died. I am grateful he died at home. I am grateful he died so peacefully. An old prayer asks God for a "death without suffering and without reproach." That was what I experienced with Gene that New Year's Day in 1998. I think what most impressed me was the naturalness of it all. I covet a death as sweet, as natural as his. Although I fought his death as if it were a strange enemy, when it appeared, it wore a familiar face.

I then remember an image and a single dream sentence I woke up with:

> You must wrap tinsel around your lamppost so
> you can really shine brighter.

Though I do not know what the implications of this are, I feel it is an encouraging, promising, uplifting way to start the New Year. I try to make sense of the dream. Figuratively, the lamp is the Word of God (Psalm 119); the omniscience of Christ (Daniel 10 and Revelation 1); salvation of God (Isaiah 62:1); God's guidance (2 Samuel 22:29); ministers and wise rulers (1 John 5:35). Light symbolizes divine wisdom and guidance. Jesus is the light of the world. There is also the association with the Sixth Chakra and is radiant energy. To "shine" implies having a whole, healed spiritual life, which would impart, disperse, and shed spiritual inspiration, knowledge, and information. When I think of tinsel, I can only relate to the tinsel we used to decorate Christmas trees with—which is what I saw in the dream, silvery, glittery, catching the light. The entire post (a Roman cross shape *T*) was wound about with the tinsel so that the light from the lamp appeared to emanate from the post, as well as reflecting it. Since the post holds the lamp, I think it could symbolize my body, which holds the light. Even in the dream, I knew I had to "reflect' on the meaning of the statement. What do I do with this? How do I comply? Is this a confirmation of my desire to be a sacrament, a reflection of God in the world?

January 2

My meditation in *Glory to Glory* is on 1 John 3:1–3, 7: "When He appears we shall be like Him."

I ask you, God, in one year, five years, twenty-five years, will I be ready for so great a transformation? I ponder this in light of the lamppost tinsel image from yesterday. I am unable to wrap myself and am utterly dependent on God. I have a will to be transformed, but God alone can accomplish that.

This eighth day of Christmas holds an unexpected gift. At nine o'clock, I receive a phone call from Sharon, who had heard me give a talk at Emmanuel Jenkins Bridge Church last April after Gene had been released from hospital. She wants to know if I would be willing to give a Cursillo Fourth Day talk on January 23 in Richmond, Virginia. My first inclination is to say, "Yes," but I tell her I need a few days to pray about it. A few days later, I wake with a dream message, "Open your mouth, and I will fill it." I think this is the answer to my prayer about going to Richmond. I feel assured that God will lead, the Spirit will move, and I will discern and follow. As I begin my early-morning meditation, asking for confirmation regarding the Fourth Day talk, I ask for a topic that God would want me to address. Immediately, into my mind flashes, "God is good, God is good all the time."

January 6

Epiphany, the twelfth day of Christmas. The meditation in *Glory to Glory* directs us to ask God to "unmask our hidden rebellions. Grace us to own our sinfulness that we may be brought to conversion, repentance, and healing. It is not our sinfulness so much that bothers God, but what we do to cover it up."

Seems a bit like the revelation I had thirty years before when it seemed that there is always forgiveness for sin because of Christ, but sin covered becomes evil, for which there is no redemption.

As if in answer to yesterday's meditation, I wake the following day with the dream image: "My sin is being revealed." I see glowing light in every dark corner. I take this as assurance that all unknown corners are being uncovered, cleansed, and forgiven. I take it as a promise of redemption and renewal by God, a Mr. Clean, who gets rid of dirt and grime and grease in just a minute.

Oh, God, I offer you my dark, my befouled, and my independence. In return, I thank you for the offering of your light and your glory.

- Cursillo was founded in Majorca, Spain in 1944. It focuses on showing Christian laypeople how to become effective Christian leaders over the course of a three-day weekend. The weekend consists of fifteen talks given by clergy and lay. The major emphasis is to ask participants to take what they have learned back into the world, on what they call the "Fourth Day." The method stresses personal spiritual development. Gene and I had attended one of these weekends four months prior to his diagnosis.

The Fourth Day

Since January 2, when Sharon asked if I would address the Cursillo community, I have been praying about it. *Do you want me to speak to Cursillo? I want to speak only your Word, God. There's no point in taking the trip to Richmond to speak* only *Barbara words.*

As the days pass, I think about where I have been and how far I have come. I am not the same person who had gone to a Cursillo weekend two and a half years before. That person had built her faith on the God of Psalm 103, who "forgives all our sins and heals all our diseases"; the God of Psalm 91, who is a deliverer, "a thousand may fall at your side, ten thousand at your right hand, but it will not come nigh unto you." That person knew the Word, had faith in the Word, stood on the Word, and clothed in Christ, felt invincible. Those passages and many others were the foundational structure on which her faith was built. They had stood her in good stead for thirty years. In the face of Gene's sudden diagnosis followed by his death nine months later, this scaffolding of her life came crashing down.

I now knew a God much bigger than my former beliefs could contain. I knew that God is good; God is good all the time. I had learned that God is in the "is," not in the "should be." God is not only in the "is," God *is* the *is*. I had lived Isaiah 41:10–13, "Fear not for I am with thee, be not afraid, for I am thy God, I will strengthen thee, I will uphold thee with the right hand of my righteousness." I had lived through the destruction of my life and had survived. God remained my steadfast friend, counselor, healer, and guide through all of my questioning, arguing, and complaining to him.

Of course, I had wanted Gene to live, wanted his life to be spared, but slowly, it dawned on me that God had not only not forsaken me but had answered a deeper desire of my heart, actually the deepest desire of my heart.

A deeper desire than Gene Fusco's life.

I remembered the first Bible Study I attended after my conversion thirty years earlier, where Philippians 3:8–11 came alive to me:

> Indeed I count everything as loss because of the surpassing worth of knowing Christ Jesus my Lord. For his sake I have suffered the loss of all things, and count them as refuse, in order that I may gain Christ and be found in him, not having a righteousness of my own, based on law, but that which is through faith in Christ, the righteousness from God that depends on faith; that I may know him and the power of his resurrection, and may share his sufferings, becoming like him in his death, that if possible I may attain the resurrection of the dead.

In the youthful fervor of early Christian life, I focused primarily on verse 10, "that I may know him and the power of his resurrection." Gene's suffering and death helped focus my mind on sharing Christ's sufferings—on God's will to conform me closer to Christ's image.

On January 23, when I stand in Saint Michaels Episcopal Church, Colonial Heights, Richmond, Virginia, to address the assembled members of the Cursillo community, I tell them about the heartache of Gene's diagnosis and death. I share with them the theological trip I had taken, the evolution of my faith, and my realization of the promise of Psalm 37:4: "If we take delight in the Lord, he will give us the desires of our heart."

One year after losing my husband, I am singing a new song. I invite them to sing a new song, to seek the Lord with all their heart, to daily rededicate themselves to his Lordship, because God is good, good all the time, because he dwells in the "is," not the "should." He demands honesty at all cost, and he can be depended on to give you the true, deepest desire of your heart.

* * * * *

Back home on lovely Chincoteague Island, the following day the meditation in *Glory to Glory* was, "Not to us, o Lord, not to us, but to your name give glory because of your kindness, because of your truth," (Psalm 115:1).

A perfect Psalm on which to meditate the morning following a standing ovation by two hundred people responding to me, loving me, and wanting to speak to me, wanting to get to know me.

"Dear God, I am not conscious of touching your glory, but you know my innermost heart. Keep me pure. Keep me clean. A broken and a contrite heart you will not despise, o God. During this past year and a half, my heart has been broken. Grant that the pieces feed a multitude."

For several days, I wake singing and happy. The Fourth Day was a gift to me, an affirmation of worth.

But the fight's not over. Soon, I return to more of the same type of spiritual and psychological struggle I've been doing since Gene's diagnosis. Not only am I searching for more inward truth, I am looking for my place in the Body of Christ—probably, if the truth be known, looking for a family. Since the Ordination Exploration Program in the Diocese of Southern Virginia involves the expenditure of several years and more money that I have, I've given up on the idea. Anyway, I have no certainty that I'm called to the priesthood, so I decide to take a two-year course in Spiritual Direction at The Well, a Roman Catholic retreat center in Smithfield, Virginia. I submit my application and Spiritual Biography to them and wait to see if I'm accepted into the program.

I've survived the first year of widowhood, wandering in the wilderness of grief on an emotional roller coaster. I will continue my search for the way to live out the purpose of my life.

Thomas Troeger tells the story of a little girl taken
to a Passion Play on good Friday by her mother.
When Jesus is crucified, the little girl gets very
upset.

"Mommy, Jesus is dead!"

"Oh, no, honey, Jesus isn't really dead. It's all right. Remember,
he comes back to life Easter morning."

The cast then carries the man on the cross down the aisle, and as
they come close to the child, she turns to her mother, "No, Mommy,
you're wrong. Jesus is dead, really dead."

When Is Dead Dead?

February 13, 1999

Following the blessings of the Fourth Day talk, I begin to carry around a heavy sadness. I seem bipolar, experiencing long periods of laughing followed by bouts of crying. Planning a trip to Arizona in three weeks to be with daughter Jeanne and my grandchildren is forcing me to experience with my body, emotions, and mind the absolute reality of Jeanne's new life. She is not coming back. Period. The feelings are similar to the finality I experienced when I had our phone number changed from Gene Fusco Plumbing to a private number. I must have hoped Gene was coming back. Because he's dead, I know that hope is insane. On the other hand, Jeanne is alive, but she's not coming back either.

Although I know I can't continue to look back, I am beginning to see I have subtly resisted living in the present—God's eternal now, kairos—by keeping Gene in my mind in an anticipation of a "heavenly future reunion." I am continuing my attachment to him. I know I have to let go. How do I do that?

Mormons teach a marriage for eternity, and Jesus says in heaven, there is no marriage. I have no proof of any future relationship for us. It might be. It might not be. But to continue to anticipate it is to continue in bondage. My life with him is over. I have to let go.

Accepting this truth makes me very sad. *God, why, oh, why, does it make me sad to be freed from an attachment? To be freed from an addiction? To be freed from a dependency?*

It's been weeks since I applied to the Well Retreat Center, in Smithfield, and I am anxious to know if I have been accepted into the Spiritual Direction program. Why, oh, why, do I need a future? Is it because my present is still impoverished?

> *Oh, God, fill me with your presence.*
> *Open my eyes to see.*
> *Open my eyes to see that the whole earth is full of your glory.*
> *Job said, "I have heard you by the hearing of my ears, but now I see you."*
> *I want to see you.*
> *I need to*
> *I will die if I don't . . .*
> *see you.*

The dream that follows these thoughts wakes me at two o'clock in the morning. I hear myself saying, "Now I wish he were dead!"

Gene has died but is alive, but he's not the Gene I know. He is mentally gone . . . drinking, smoking, grossly overweight, his skin very dark. We are facing financial destruction. He is behaving inappropriately with his daughter, and I want to kill him! Not only did he destroy our life with his self-destructive behaviors, but this behavior is beyond the pale. I throw a knife at his head. He gets very angry. We fight. "Now I wish he were dead," rings loud and clear.

As bad as it may be to want to kill your husband who has returned from the dead, I feel very good about this dream. Although I was angry in the dream, awake I feel uplifted and encouraged. Reflecting on yesterday's anticipation of a heavenly reunion as a last-ditch hope for a "happily ever after" ending, I believe that my willingness to kill Gene indicates my willingness to kill my fantasies and live in the present, in reality. I sure hope so.

* * * * *

March comes in like a lion, a whippin' up the water in the bay.

While cleaning a closet yesterday, I found the video we had made when Gabriela was born. Gene was reading a book to our grandson, Lucas. So sweet, the two of them on the floor in Lucas's bedroom. The video ends March 9, 1997, just three weeks before Gene went to hospital. I hurt to a depth I haven't since the day Gene died. I went for a long, hard, fast walk. Very hurt and very angry. I wanted to have a temper tantrum, throw something, break things. Unbearable to see all of us together like that, and now never to be again. God!

Many windy days follow. The wind. The hostile, wicked wind wakes me at three in the morning, chasing all dream images out of my mind. The wind still engenders in me the feeling of desolation that overwhelmed me the night I came home after leaving Gene in hospital. Bereft. I hear the old windows rattle. I hear the shingles fly off the roof. I am acutely aware of the magnitude of my need and the limit of my resources. The wind reminds me of my total helplessness to ever begin to appropriate your gifts, blessings, graces, and love, oh, God. The wind reminds me of my vulnerability, my naked exposure to sorrow, suffering, loss, and yes, even the elements.

Oh, my God, I need you so. You are the Lord of my life. You are the Lord of my downcast emotions. You are the way, the truth, and the life. You said, "I am the way: we will walk it together; I am the truth: we will experience it together; I am your life: we will live it together." Immerse me anew in your Holy Spirit, who is light to cast out my darkness . . . who is fullness of life to renew my life . . . who is fullness of love to flood my heart with love for you.

* * * *

On Monday, March 8, I must leave for New Jersey as Laura and I are flying to Arizona tomorrow.

Tuesday, aboard the plane, I feel peaceful and happy. Although I know the take-off is a dangerous part of the flight, I love the sensation. We had prepared sandwiches and snacks of raisins, carrots, and apples. As I look out of the window at the intensely blue sky, I can hardly believe that I am thirty thousand feet in the air. I appear to be standing still. Overcoming the law of gravity, like overcoming the problems of the world by the Law of the Spirit of the Life in Christ, is mind-boggling. I have a lovely feeling of detachment, of timelessness. I'm in a World War II movie, peering out of a little window. Time stands still as I race into the future.

God, grant me the grace to remain in the moment, to live in kairos.

Our reunion with Jeanne at the airport feels like we've never been apart. She, Laura, and I are so happy to be together again. However, the following week, as we attempt to get acquainted with her "new" family, is laced with misunderstandings, tensions, and unresolved past issues. At the end of the week, when she returns us to the airport, she drops us off two and a half hours before we needed to be there. It's an extreme example of, "Here's your hat what's your hurry." Laura and I are heartbroken. As quickly as Gene was taken from us, and as far apart from one another as we now live, this could be the last time we see each other, and everything about Jeanne says, "Get on your way, I have to be about my day!" It seems there is no place for us in her life. *God grant me the grace of forgiveness. Grant me detachment.*

*****

I took several notebooks to Arizona but was so out of touch with myself that I ended up making no journal entries during the entire trip. Upon my return to New Jersey, I was thrilled with green. Dry, brown, hot Arizona gave me a whole new perspective on the beauty of the Garden State. I was very happy to be back East. So happy, that is, except for my ears. The ear pain I experienced while landing remained for a week. Flying is something I shall not be doing very often. I stay at Laura's house for several days, do some shopping, and have lunch with a friend. Friday afternoon, I leave for Virginia and spend Saturday readjusting. Sunday morning, I do not want to go to church. I do not want to answer, "How was Arizona?" a multitude of times. How often can I say, "Dry"? And I certainly don't want to rehash the emotional wounds. I stay home and spend the afternoon watching the cleansing, renewing rain outside my window. God, the rain is wonderful.

The laughing gulls return between 9:00 p.m. and 3:00 a.m. on the last day of March. Without them, the winter is very quiet, and then, all of a sudden, thousands of them arrive simultaneously with loud, raucous shouts. Since the dream Laura had when Gene was a huge white bird, she sees him in all birds. Is he playing a part in their arrival on the second anniversary of our descent into the valley of the shadow of death?

"Whenever I've seen a collapsed lung like this, the tumor is malignant. You have family in New Jersey. I think you should go back there."

A little after sunrise, I go sit on the back porch to soak up the warmth of the spring sun and rejoice in God's power to create, recreate, and heal.

I do love you, God. I thank you for my life and my health. You are the Lord of all creation.

* * * * *

April 1, Maundy Thursday

Go to church and take away from the sermon a powerful thought, pertinent for this time in my life. Based on Henri Nowen's, *Can You Drink This Cup*, I see how we must share our cup of suffering as well as our cup of joy. It's easy to share one another's joy. Not so easy to share suffering, but intimacy grows in the soil of suffering. When we share joy, we have a barrier, a sense of control. When we share suffering, the barriers are destroyed. We are vulnerable and bond soul to soul, spirit to spirit. I see there is reason to be thankful for my sorrow.

I am grieving more since the Arizona trip, struggling with my prayer time, less conscious of the presence of God. One evening, in the midst of the pain, a walk on the beach lifts my spirits. The ocean seems full of the glory of God, like millions of diamonds rolling up on the beach. If God is all in all and the whole world reflects his glory, how dare we say the sparkling, ever-changing lights are only a reflection of the moon? It is an awesome sight.

April 4, Easter

Alleluia, the Lord is risen. The Lord is risen, indeed. If we have died with him, we shall also be raised with him! Joyful Easter morning to you, Gene. Joyful day of resurrection!

April 6

Beginning the *Spiritual Exercises of Ignatius*, I am reminded of my attachment to the members of my family. Though the past was not perfect, certainly not pain-free, my attachment was strong. I passionately loved my husband and children. However, attachment can become slavery, a ball and chain. Right now I'm not sure where love fits into it this, but the introduction to the *Spiritual Exercises* has brought me face-to-face, again, to attachment, and I am being led to see more deeply where my soul is presently residing. I want to be free to live, to give all of myself to God. I don't want to live in attachment. Neither do I want to live in a protective detachment attempting to save myself from pain.

Dear God, illumination please.

In the afternoon, I take a long nap.

Ten minutes after I wake, Jeanne calls. She's all excited because after a long drought, Arizona received an inch of rain in April. I did feel a bit like Elijah, praying for rain, while I was there. Actually, the first bit of rain began as Laura and I flew out of Las Vegas. She tells me, "All the mountains around the valley are snow-covered. Sunday we drove to Superior and played in the snow! Imagine, in April. Flagstaff had one-and-a-half feet and the Grand Canyon had three."

"My, that must be beautiful." I say, remembering how much I enjoyed Flagstaff and the Canyon in March.

A slight pause leads to, "Mom, I loved having you here. I couldn't go into the airport because it was too painful, not because I was indifferent to your leaving. I also know I have work issues. I need to solve them. They consume me."

"You are so much like your father in this regard. It can be self-destructive, you know," I comment.

"After I left you off at the airport, I said to myself, I am becoming just like Daddy, and I don't want to do that to Lucas and Gabriela!"

"You don't want to do it to me and Laura either."

A wonderful aspect of this conversation is that she had not one defensive note in her voice over this "problem" of becoming like Dad. I am very blessed by this exchange. Often Gene seemed to see the truth about himself but then seemed to lack the power to change, to walk in a new way. *God Almighty, grant Jeanne the power. Amen.*

No more than ten minutes after Jeanne and I say, "Good-bye. I love you. I love you too," Laura calls. She's confused about a beautiful love-sister-friend Easter card she has received from Jeanne.

"Mom, was the Arizona trip a figment of my imagination? Was it as bad as I remember?"

Having just spoken to Jeanne, I could assure Laura, "The truth is we are perfect in Christ, but we don't often act in accord with that truth. The truth is Jeanne loves us and does not always act in accord with that truth. We must accept by faith the truth."

Trips to New Jersey fill much of the next several weeks. The "house of promise" that we built in 1981 is under contract. Negotiations have been going on for several months, and I receive a call today informing me the closing is in a week and requires my presence at the attorney's office in Jamesburg. I recall how Gene depended on that house to be his retirement fund. How ironic that the sale comes when he is no longer here. The closing will mark the end of all things connected with Gene and our life in New Jersey.

Betty, seventeen years older than I, my best friend and sister soul mate, is having health issues. She has begun bleeding from the rectum and fears another surgery. I start thinking about future possible problems and how I might handle them. My mother is eighty-three and may not continue to be independent. Many times I have asked her to move to Virginia with me. She refuses.

When I think about Betty and my mother, I feel empty. I have nothing to say. I have nothing to give. Remembering what Gene went through, I complain to God, "If I, a sinful person, would not wish what he went through on my worst enemy, how could you do that to your child? How could you let this happen to your child?"

Round and round I go in my angry accusations.

After a while, I hear God quietly say, "Look at my son."

Yes, God, I need to do that. I need to look at Jesus. In great depth and at great length. God, increase in me the word of wisdom and the word of understanding. That is the only way that I can begin to get a handle on any of this and function as your sacrament in this world.

I have been conscious these past days of, not so much being full of evil, but of being empty of good.

Facing so many unknowns. Having so few answers.

One morning I begin my Bible reading with Jeremiah 10:23, "O Lord I know that the way of a man is not in himself; it is not in man, even a strong man or a man at his best, to direct his own steps. Oh, Lord, correct, instruct, chastise me, but with judgment and in just measure, not in your anger, lest you diminish me."

Here is the guidance I am looking for, the answer to my questions. Will I need to do something for Betty? For my mother? Will I have time to spend with Laura, who is facing divorce?

Even though I have no specific answers, Jeremiah frees me on a deep level. I accept that I don't have the power or ability or whatever to direct my path. So I am off the hook, so to speak. Ah, but can I really trust God? Is God good? Does he love me? You see, I don't want to suffer. I really don't. And I still equate goodness and love with my comfort level, and I see fear and suffering and sickness on every side. Because I have experienced being grief-stricken and God blesses me, fills me, and provides for me, I don't understand why I am so afraid today. Is it because too many old attachments are being shaken at one time—the house of promise, Betty, my mother, and Laura? In spite of the fact that my mind and my spirit reassure me there is nothing to fear, my emotions give me a different message. *God, speak peace to my quaking emotions.*

During these struggles with attachments and detachments, my friend Emily says to me before I leave for New Jersey to go the closing, "I have never seen your face look like this before . . . apart and resolute, with deep, deep sadness in your eyes."

"I'm beyond words," I tell her. "It's not that I don't want to sell the house, I do. I am just beyond words."

She wants to stay with me, she wants to help, but I feel myself backing away. There is no help to be found in this world. In fact, in spirit I have already left Virginia.

Going to bed late, I sleep fitfully.

* * * * *

April 12

The closing on the house on Gravel Hill Spotswood Road goes smoothly. I visit Betty to offer support and pray with her. Laura gives me a massage. I have pain and tears in my chest (heart?) and feel lost and inept. Several nights, I dream of rain (tears?). Three days later, I decide to leave for home.

Back home I feel like I look like an atom in motion—touching Emily's life, Laura's life, my mother's life, and Betty's life—while belonging nowhere and to no one.

When does all this grieving cease? I have no one but you.

> *You* are the Lord of my life
> You are the *Lord* of my life.
> You are the Lord of my *life*.
> You are my *Father*, my *Husband*, my *Bridegroom*.
> This is your house.
> The money I received on Monday is your money.

It is not only that I offer again all of this to you but that I remember the truth of my life, who I am and who you are. I ask you to baptize me anew with the Holy Spirit, the spirit of peace, of truth, of joy, of wisdom, of understanding.

I wake the following day feeling optimistic and aware of the love of God. *Thank you, thank you.* The world is shrouded in dense, beautiful fog that obliterates the end of the dock. I renew my prayers for an increase of the Holy Spirit. I don't ask for an increase of tongues because I see no value in it, just like I see no value in what Gene went through.

Suddenly, I'm convicted, because after all, what do I know?

What do I know?

I open *Glory to Glory* for my morning meditation, and what do I read?

> Forgive us for all the ways that we have used our minds that could now block the gift of vision. Thank you for forgiving us. In the name of Jesus, with the blood of Jesus, we free our minds to receive the visions that you would give us for our lives and our church today.

Wow, isn't that what I just said to you earlier, "Because I don't see the value of tongues or Gene's suffering or whatever." Wow. What do I know, anyway? *Free my mind, renew my mind so that I don't block your Words to me.*

I am on the porch reading, and the first hummingbird shows up at 12:30 p.m. This scout always comes a few days before the rest of them. *I thank you, God, for this peaceful backyard that is a sanctuary for yellow and purple finches, pine siskins, sparrows, cardinals, and now the delightful hummingbirds.*

I receive a letter from Jeanne containing a copy of a poem she had written April 24, a year ago on her birthday. It's about the loss of her father. Tore me up. Squeezed my heart almost to death. Such pain for all of us. She ends the poem with the thought that she and Gene have both lost a lot and won a lot and for now, they are both free. Oh, dear God, show us what we have won, show us our freedom.

Before bed, I'm reading Isaiah 30:18–21, and encouraged, I begin to sing,

The Lord is waiting to show you favor,
he rises to pity you;
he will be gracious to you when you cry out,
as soon as he hears, he will answer you.

Thinking about Jeanne and her new family . . . remembering
how I felt when Lucas was all excited about going to "Grampa Bob's"
for his birthday. Oh, how easily Gene has been replaced. I know, I
know, it's better the child has a family, but I feel I've given them all
out for adoption. What do I do? How can I handle this? I can't deal
with their death because they're not dead. They also are not "alive" in
my life. God, I don't know where to put them. To remain attached
is to suffer continuously. To let them go totally seems to put them
to death. I don't know where to put them. I didn't ask for them,
never particularly wanted children. God gave them. Then God took
them away, like Isaac was given to Abraham. I don't know where to
put them. Into God's hands on the altar, I guess. But even Abraham
knew within a few days of the start of the trip to Moriah what the
outcome was. I can't see the outcome, and it will be years before I
know who died, the child or the ram. I know when I put Gene on the
altar, I took him back many times. Maybe it will be easier to release
them because I see and interact with them so rarely. I don't know. I
just don't know.

I open *Glory to Glory*, and the meditation for today is Luke 9:6:
"This is what the Lord orders you to do that the glory of the Lord
may be revealed to you. Come up to the altar and offer your sin offering and your holocaust for you and your family." Timely, I must say.

I go on to read 1 Peter 2, "He himself bore my sins in his body
on the tree, so that free from sin I might live for righteousness."

The passage begins with suffering justly and unjustly. My sin
offering is Jesus Christ crucified, so if I am justified through Christ, I
believe I must no longer suffer for my wrongdoing. God, please plant
that deep in my soul and let me not forget it.

April 26

The rest of the hummingbirds arrive this morning at nine forty-five.

I am reading *Changed into His Likeness* by Watchman Nee. He has a meditation on the God of Abraham, Isaac and Jacob. Abraham signifies that God *chooses* us through no merit of our own, as Abraham was an idolater among idolaters.

The principle of Isaac's life is *receiving*. He symbolizes the life God makes available to us in the gift of his Son. Jacob is notable for his suffering and the disciplinary work of the Holy Spirit. He is the principle of *natural strength*. We cannot achieve God's ends by our own efforts. Thus, the Spirit moves to attain God's ends by his own means. He *chooses* us, *gifts* us with his son, and *cuts short* our old, self-willed nature to make way for our new nature in Christ. Circumstances are God's appointments for our good. First Peter 1:6–7 tells me there is nothing accidental in my life. It is all measured out to me. I may not welcome the discipline, but it is designed, in the end, to make me a partaker in God's holiness. My natural life has a nerve center, a life principle—which I usually do not recognize but which God takes pains to point out—and this is my personal Peniel where I am painfully crippled. I must remember God never preached to Jacob. He simply gave him promises and, without stopping to exhort or explain, went to work on him. This shows me that the natural strength cannot be changed by doctrine; it can be changed only by the chastening of God! *May I hold still for your chastening, Lord.*

I soon have a dream that I later analyze and find encouraging . . .

A group of us are in church, and "they" asked me to lead the prayer. I begin, "O Lord God Almighty, for you are all and you are mighty and you are all power, might, and glory. Because you are the total and complete, there is nothing outside you . . ." Then I begin to lose my train of thought, get off track, get distracted, because "they" were giving gifts to me and Gene.

The gifts are in long, narrow boxes, and as Gene opens the first one, I see a long feather boa. I consider the gift inappropriate and useless and wonder why, in God's name, "they" had given it to us.

What with Gene sick and all, we need food and money to pay our bills a lot more than this useless, very expensive boa.

After recording the dream, I begin to ponder its meaning. Looking up definitions, I learn that a huge boa is a snake. The boa has no venom; it crushes its victim. The snake takes me to the Garden of Eden, sin, Satan, etc., but when I look up snake in a dictionary of dream symbols, I find this:

> Snake/Serpent = Kundalini, the creative life force
> raising one to spiritual awareness.

Carl Jung says it is the most significant symbol related to the renewal of human personality. It is the oldest Christ spirit symbol. In Numbers 21:9, Moses lifted up the serpent on the pole in the wilderness, and everyone who looked upon it was saved and healed. It is the origin of the medical symbol, the caduceus. In alchemy, it is mercury, quicksilver—which represents the driving life forces of living, dying, rebirth. Snakes represent basic spine, lower brain, right brain, autonomic nervous system. When we begin to touch them with consciousness, as we do in dreams, new functions are added to our consciousness.

Well, well, well.

I think I see in the dream that I was way too practical and earthbound by thinking food for the body was more important than the gift of the boa, and it seems that I was resisting change. But now that I am awake and conscious, I want to receive this wonderful feather boa—which, I recall, was blue, green, and white.

I begin to pray, asking God to open my eyes, ears, heart, and mind to the innovative, the creative, the impossible, and enable me to let loose of old ideas that are no longer useful for me now. Also, I remember the previous day I was reflecting on expectant faith, and the snake often denotes pregnancy. It seems possible that I am pregnant with new life. I certainly hope so.

I praise God each morning for the natural beauty that surrounds me. I continue prayer and study. I read spiritual classics, psychology books, and find help in the Enneagram, which I discover is a map to my psyche. Laura shares the body-mind-spirit connection from her fund of knowledge. I'm making progress, but sometimes I'm taken by surprise with the acute awareness that Gene is gone, as if some deep part of me is learning this for the first time. *When is dead dead, I wonder.* I like solitude and feel I need it to seek God to hasten my healing, but I spend a lot of time dancing with the demons of loneliness.

I remain involved in church work, composing and delivering sermons, reading the lessons in Emily's churches and in mine. I accompany her on pastoral visits. Several people come to me for counseling. The Well has accepted me into its Spiritual Direction program, and once a month, I cross the Chesapeake Bay Bridge Tunnel on my way to Smithfield for the weekend. I perceive my home now as a combination university-convent, a healing home, and it pleases me.

I keep busy working part-time in three different shops. On one of my walks to work, I notice large slabs of broken concrete along the side of the road. *I could use that for fill on my waterfront.* Several days later, I see a man in the yard near it and stop to ask if I may have it. He is happy to give it to me. I go home, get the Chrysler Town and Country van, and make three trips to load and cart it home. Heavy work—the slabs were twenty to sixty pounds apiece. That evening I take a hot bath, hoping to prevent soreness. Though sore the next day, I determine to walk through the doors that God opens and receive the gifts he provides.

* * * * *

Two weeks of humidity, haze, and suffocating air usher in September, and I am weighted down, pressed down in spirit. Hurricane Dennis has barely dissipated, and Floyd, organizing himself in the south, is not far behind. *I am all out of kilter, God. Search my heart and reveal my spirit to me. What is the cause of this malaise, this disease?* Since it's raining, I decide to clear a cabinet to make room for things I'm using now. I uncover trivial things that stir my memories. I am overcome with horror and disbelief that Gene is really gone. Another of an endless series of levels that just now realizes the facts of our life. And this pain is one tiny drop of the pain in millions of hearts right now, and in billions throughout time. It's unbelievable. Unbearable.

God, how do you bear it? How do I?

> Daily I turn to my Rock, my Fortress, my Savior.
> My life feels like a Psalm . . .

> God save me from my enemies; the water is up
> to my neck . . .

> Yet I will praise him; glory to the Lord of Hosts.

> I can't bear the pain; I'm dying . . .

> He has turned my mourning into joy.

* * * * *

Jeanne calls, and after a lovely chat, Lucas wants to talk to me. I had received a finger painting by Gabriela on which Lucas had added a stick figure family. I had guessed the adults were his mother, father, and Mr. Mark (Jeanne's second husband). When I thanked him for the picture, he told me the people were his mom, Tia (aunt) Laura, and me.

"I squeezed Mr. Mark in later," he said.

Obviously, Laura and I are some kind of stable, constant force in his life.

> Oh, Gene

> How he needs you

> A man in his life who thinks he's just wonderful

> who has no obligation for his daily training.

> Oh, Gene

> Lucas had gone fourteen months without seeing
> Laura and me

> so how does he comprehend that you are dead?

Looking into the Void

Iris had a stroke November 2 and three days later was dead. I am deeply affected by the loss of my dearest friend at church. We were near the same age, and based on the longevity of our mothers, we thought we'd have twenty more years together. How presumptuous. For almost two years, I have tried to make sense of Gene's death. I can find no explanation for Iris passing away so suddenly. We connected on a deep spiritual level, and she loved God as I did. Her death is opening old wounds in me. I feel betrayed, deceived.

I saw the movie *Gaslight* when I was nine and was indelibly impressed with the dread and horror of not being able to trust the person you love and live with. Thinking about deception and dread makes me uncomfortable, so I allow myself to be distracted by the surreal colors in front of my house. I go to the back to check the east for a vivid sunrise and, finding none, return to the west facing porch. I see vivid, blue clear sky. Long level stripes of deep pink clouds. Olive and golden marsh grasses. Taupe and gray rough water. The scene begins to change into lavender, rose, and pure white above a wisteria sky in less than sixty seconds. The water is now assuming a deep aquamarine shade.

Wow, oh, wow, oh, wow.

I am not only distracted by the beauty of you and your creation. I am overwhelmed by the magnitude of that which is presenting itself to me. Soon the colors calm, and all is mauve, and I emotionally resume deception thoughts.

In my world
in my reality
constructed of timbers of truth
You betrayed me
when it all came crashing down
You deceived me
You said, "I am the God that healeth thee"
You said Psalm 91 and 103
You said, "I will lay none of these diseases on you"
You said, "The Kingdom is healing and deliverance"
You said, "The deaf hear, the lame walk."
I know you are a man of your word
You deceived me.
Gene.
Iris.
Gram.
All struck down young
You deceived me
Tears . . . tears . . . tears
Please show me your world
Invite me into your world
Let me dwell in your world
I want to know its timbers
I want to experience its truth
I think I am the little salt doll
who enters the ocean/God
and disappears.
I don't know you
I can't handle you
any more than I can handle the moment by moment panorama of changing colors outside my window
an ever-new

ever-creative
ever-beautiful
ever-mysterious display.

I am stunned by this outpouring almost two years after Gene's death.

I have a basic fear of being overwhelmed by God. I'm sad, lethargic, and heavyhearted. I am afraid. Oh, God, I am so afraid of you, of uncertainty, of total helplessness. I am so afraid of the fact that there is nothing I can do to make life safe. I'm scared of the void, the end of human experience. Since Gene's death, the void has often overwhelmed me. How often I have said, "I can't believe he's gone, has ceased to be." I tell myself there is eternal life, but that doesn't satisfy my problem of loss and pain. He—as a flesh and blood, self-conscious person, with his magnificent singing voice, his repertoire of jokes—is gone.

So I tell myself he's not really dead. If I can experience the void here in my body, on earth, can Gene experience self-awareness there, bodiless, in heaven? Can he be happy in the void? I believe in eternal life.

Jesus said, "He who lives and believes in me shall never die."

We are not destroyed after death. We shall have a new name and a resurrection body. Does not the scripture say we shall know him because we shall be like him? The split must be healed, soul and spirit, finite and infinite, solid and vapor. Psychologists tell us that our unconscious has a very real sense of its eternal nature and life after physical death, but our conscious mind, our ego, struggles. I believe God is calling me into the void. *Help me not to put up a fuss.*

* * * * *

It's four o'clock in the morning. The moon is taking my breath away . . . huge, fat, orange-gold cutting a wide swath across the bay. Glorious. Will death be such a glorious trip into undreamed beauties provided we have relinquished all so the pain of separation doesn't mar the trip?

135

Approaching Holidays

Dreams after Iris's death are filled with strife, stress, and conflict. Life is heavy. I'd like to skip over the approaching holidays and get on with the New Year. I am longing for my family, and longing hurts like hell. When Laura's divorce is final, I fear she may move to Arizona to be near her nephew, Lucas, whom she adores. I feel her pain, in addition to my own, as the last threads of our family are unraveling.

Thanksgiving Day, I'm awake at one thirty and hope to leave for Laura's around three o'clock.

> For fifty-six years I woke to the smell of turkey
> For thirty-four years I cooked turkey
> At times I cooked for thirty-five people
> So this is different.
> This is good.
> To everything there is a season.
> I love you, God
> Thank you for my life
> Use me to usher in your kingdom.

I arrive in New Jersey around seven in the morning. In the afternoon, we visit my eighty-three-year-old mother in her efficiency apartment—after which, Laura and I have a Thanksgiving Day sandwich at a local diner. We share our love for one another. We share our grief with one another. I stay in New Jersey five days. We visit my niece, Terri, who tells me, "Aunt Bobbi, I always felt you were in a holding pattern when you were married. I thought Uncle Gene would die before you and that you'd have a whole other life." She must have been a teenager at the time. I never knew she felt that way. It seems she was prophetic. I never felt in a holding pattern, though. My life was my home and family. I felt it was my purpose, my calling.

Home the following week, I feel flat, emotionless, except for sadness. I miss Laura terribly.

God, I need you. Restore to me the joy of my salvation. Bless Laura, watch over her, and guide her through this time of transition. Inspire, enlighten, speak, and give me ears to hear.

Following this prayer, I have two unforgettable dreams.

Working with Dreams

I'm including the two dreams that follow, and the active imagination work I did with them, because I think they illustrate the work of God in the subconscious in the individuation process, in the cultivation of the Christ wholeness—or whatever theological/psychological terminology one prefers. Jesus knew the heart of every man, and I don't think that means in the way we know people, such as, "She has such a good heart." I believe he knew all—conscious, subconscious, unconscious. After all, did he not become man, and did he not know himself, and did he not know God?

Active Imagination Dialogue is a technique developed by Jung to help amplify, interpret, and integrate the contents of dreams. When approached by way of writing, active imagination is like writing a play. One takes a figure that appears in a dream and starts to converse with the figure in writing. One challenges the dream figure and lets him/her challenge the dreamer. "Why are you in my dream?" "Who are you?" "What do you want from me?" And so on. A dialogue ensues. This technique helps recover rejected, unknown parts and makes them available to the ego and consciousness. With practice, the dreamer can become accomplished at expressing the various points of view, just as a playwright does.

* * * * *

Dream 1

December7, 1999

I am soaking a duck in salt water. I (*It*} is skinned, eyes frozen shut, and has a long tail—which breaks off when I turn it over in the water. I notice it is not gutted. I think it ought to be, but I do not do it. Gene comes along and begins pouring cornmeal or barley or some other grain into the water, and I question him on this. He says the duck isn't fresh; it's stale. "Can't you smell it?" "No, I hadn't noticed." As a result (I guess) of the thawing and the grain, the eyes begin to open. "Oh my god, it's not dead. I am so sorry that I let some damage come to it, and I am so glad that I didn't gut it." When it becomes fully awake, it is no longer a duck. I'm not sure of the body because I remain fixated on the eyes. As I keep looking at them, they become almond shaped and alert in a face similar to an Abyssinian cat, long and narrow with short hair, taupe gray in color.

* * * * *

Since I wrote I rather than It (Freudian slip?) referring to the frozen duck, I will take the tack that I am
the frozen duck, and I become the live cat.

Active Imagination ala Jung—I quiet myself, pic-
ture the duck, the dialog begins.

Me: Duck with those frozen closed eyes that look like parrot eyes, who are you? Are you me?

Duck: Yes.

Me: I am so glad I didn't gut you and put you in warm salt water.

Duck: I'm not. It was painful.

Me: Yes, to live is painful.

Duck: I know, but it's okay, it really is.

Me: Well, I'm glad about that. How did you become cat?

Duck: . . . (*Silence.*)

Me: Cat, who are you?

Cat: I am your deepest instinct.

Me: What can I do to nurture you and learn from you?

Cat: Well, I'm so glad that you asked that question.

> (Up until now, I hadn't been sure it was a cat, for I had focused only on its eyes and face. It had been sitting very straight, facing me. At this point, it stretches, gets up and takes a long step to its left. Its body is long and slender, like a wild cat.)

Me: You are a very slim, powerful cat, not at all like the type I cuddle. Teach me. (He turns his head and acknowledges me, but no talk.)

> Cat, will you please talk to me? Ah, I see you are as independent as a cat. (*I find myself smiling.*) Cat, I don't want to try to force you to talk to me. Obviously, if you are my deepest intuition, I can expect you to communicate with me that way, an intuitive way. Am I right?"

Cat: . . . (*Smiles.*)

Me: In a flash, you could be the lion of the tribe of Judah, couldn't you? I think it's possible you are an essential part of the Sixth Chakra, third eye, my wisdom, my intuition, or whatever label you want to call it. I value you. I want to grow in my relationship with you. I don't want to run off, but I need to take a shower and prepare for the meeting I have this morning. I have become energized during this conversation and touched by your willingness to speak with me. Thank you.

Cat: (*Stretches out in one of those regal sphinx postures on a hearth or rug. I know Cat is staying; he's not going anywhere. He lays his head down, and I sense I can get on with my day.*)

Dream 2

December 9, 1999

My daughter Jeanne and I are walking in the marsh and notice a duck trying to distract us (as a killdeer might do to protect her young). "She must have a nest nearby, and maybe we've harmed it." We retrace our steps and find a nest well camouflaged. There appears to be at least a dozen baby ducks in the nest. Jeanne goes closer to investigate, reaches down to pick one up, and lo and behold, it is a cat. I keep telling her not to touch them because the mother will probably abandon them. She ignores me and picks up a patterned cat, white with gray, black, blue sketching on it like a pen and ink drawing. Even though we had thought these were babies, this is a good-sized cat, maybe twenty pounds. There is an entire nest of snuggly, curled-together cats. We are familiar with the pattern on the cat, but . . . now awake, I don't remember what we called it.

God, oh, God, what is this symbolism? First the dead, skinned, frozen duck comes alive into a cat. Now, tonight, a live duck is mothering and raising an entire nest of cats. What is the connection between ducks and cats?

I attempt to quiet myself, meditate, and pray. I am sensing God's presence and also my sorrow over Gene two years ago this month. In no way do I see a connection between cats and ducks, so I will attempt to immerse myself in the cat of last night. I visualize it in Jeanne's arms, head toward her left, in conformation like an adult white tiger; but rather than tiger markings, it had a symbol on its side from shoulder to its tail, the symbol we had a name for in the dream.

Active Imagination Dialogue

Me: As big as you are, you are still a baby. I don't even know if you can walk yet. (*He is looking at me intently. So trusting, so wise, so beautiful. He is still in her arms.*) You are so beautiful.

Cat: (*Keeping his eyes on me, he squirms to get free from her grasp. He's getting taller and more regal looking. He is now full grown and loping toward me with his eyes fixed on mine. He races toward, me, takes a final leap, and disappears into me. I am a little apprehensive and excited at this point. I feel heat in my solar plexus, or Third Chakra area. He seems to fit in me like those designs on the back of Oriental kimonos.*)

I now have two spirit cats in my life: the long skinny Abyssinian, (my deepest intuition) and this white tiger (who exudes power, strength, and single-minded confidence)—a very strange affair for an orthodox, Bible-believing Christian.

One was brought to life by Gene's grain, the harvest of his life.

One was brought to life by a maternal, protective duck. The duck, as a bird, could represent spirit and the higher self. Swimming on the surface of the water, it symbolizes what is in the conscious mind. Diving, it probes the depths of the unconscious. Dream birds can represent the opening up of the higher self, or the attainment of enlightenment.

The following night I sleep nine peaceful hours with no dream recall.

> I wake full of joy and praising God.
> I feel exhilarated, full of elixir!
> I love you, God.
> I thank you for my life.
> I thank you for my joy.
> I thank you for my purpose.

Each morning, as I enter into centering prayer, I invite the Abyssinian and the white tiger to be with me and am conscious during the day of their presence with me and their gifts to me.

We must be willing to get rid of the life we had planned, so as to have the life that is waiting for us. (Joseph Campbell)

I believe we have two lives—the life we learn with and the life we live after that. (Movie, *The Natural*)

> Humans are born soft and supple;
> dead they are stiff and hard.
> Plants are born tender and pliant,
> dead, they are brittle and dry.
> Thus, whoever is still and inflexible
> is a disciple of death.
> Whoever is soft and yielding
> is a disciple of life.
>
> (Chap. 76 Lao-tz, S. Mitchell)

Winter

The month of December used to be filled with baking cookies and fruitcakes, planning menus for entertaining, and wrapping presents. Not now.

I spend much time in prayer and meditation. I have a picture of the still center of myself and the transitory nature of emotion, both pleasant and unpleasant. Perfect and purrfect with Abyssinian and tiger.

I sing "Saint Patrick's Breastplate" . . . "I bind unto myself today, the strong name of the Trinity . . ." and I want to sign myself with the cross from head to toe, and fingertip to fingertip of outstretched arms.

The Song of Zechariah, the song of praise of God's deliverance, speaks life to me:

> Blessed be the Lord God of Israel,
> for he hath visited and redeemed his people;
> And hath raised up a mighty salvation for us
> in the house of his servant David,
> As he spake by the mouth of his holy prophets,
> which have been since the world began:
> That we should be saved from our enemies,
> and from the hand of all that hate us;
> To perform the mercy promised to our forefathers,
> and to remember his holy covenant;

To perform the oath which he sware to our fore-
father Abraham,
that he would give us,
That we being delivered out of the hand of our
enemies
might serve him without fear,
in holiness and righteousness before him,
all the days of our life.
And thou, child, shall be called the prophet of
the Highest,
for thou shalt go before the face of the Lord to
prepare his ways;
To give knowledge of salvation unto his people
for the remission of their sins,
Through the tender mercy of our God,
whereby the dayspring from on high hath visited
us;
To give light to them that sit in darkness
and in the shadow of death,
and to guide our feet into the way of peace.

I have an overwhelming sense of God's presence and peace as
the world prepares to celebrate the coming of the Prince of Peace. I
have nothing to fear. God is able to birth a mature Son of God within
me, and I can't help him in any way, other than Mary's way, "Do it
unto according to your will."

*Do with me what you want. Thy will be done. I
want your will above all else in life.*

Christmas Eve, I drive back to New Jersey to
spend time with Laura, my mother, and Betty.

Christmas morning, John 3:33 and 34:

Anyone who believes Jesus, discovers that God is a fountain of truth.

A fountain! I can anticipate living water to continuously wash over me forever and reveal more areas I need to have cleansed. There is no room for discouragement. Of course, I will always see more areas that have been hiding in the darkness. I'm anticipating them to be revealed in the light of truth and being changed from glory to glory, as I behold him with unveiled face with no mask, no pretense, no self-deception, no shame, no avoidance. The discovery of these dark places will become an occasion for rejoicing rather than the shameful condemnation I have known in the past. Each step will bring me closer to my goal, my heart's desire, to be conformed to Christ. *Thank you, God, for the presents of your presence.*

I think I feel ready to spend next Christmas with Jeanne and her family. I'm presuming a lot. Will we all be alive? Will the earth still be here? Who knows? I needed last Christmas alone on my beloved island, but I feel stirrings of joy and anticipation thinking about next year.

I go home on the thirtieth and wait for Y2K.

The doomsayers are predicting the end of our life, as we know it.

January 1, 2000

A new century, a new millennium, and the second anniversary of Gene passing out of this world into the next. God bless you as you go from glory to glory, sweetheart.

I praise God for heat, electricity, and good coffee. The predicted catastrophe doesn't materialize. As midnight rolls from country to country, time zone to time zone, celebrations go on without a hitch.

Sing to God, Defender of Widows. He gives the solitary a home and brings forth prisoners into freedom (Psalms 68).

All shall be well,
and all shall be well,
and manner of thing shall be well.

—Julian of Norwich

Spring

It is spring. Three years have passed since your death sentence was pronounced and we were told to go back to New Jersey.

I am so grateful we stayed put. Where else but here on Chincoteague could I have found peace and hope?

I look down at my left hand holding open a book and see my college ring on my third finger. I realize I'm okay. Gene, you have left me okay. Look at my home. Look at my books. Look at the beauty of this spring day. Gene, you left me not just okay; you left me better than okay. I wore this ring before I wore our wedding ring, and I've been wearing it for months now. It signifies where my heart is: the pursuit of wisdom. My focus is on my *true* self, my *eternal* self, my glory, my light . . . and yours too, sweetheart. I've left behind my desperate need for you and for my family.

I am okay.

No more grieving for what isn't.

About the Author

An only child, she grew up on a farm in New Jersey, where her love of nature was evident from the beginning.

Upon earning a BS degree from East Stroudsburg University, Pennsylvania, in 1963, she met Eugene Fusco, whom she married six weeks later.

In their twenty-fifth year of marriage, after raising two daughters, they fulfilled a lifelong dream of living by the water and moved to Chincoteague Island, Virginia.

She remarried after seventeen years of widowhood and currently divides her time between Chincoteague Island, Virginia and Bordentown, New Jersey.

CPSIA information can be obtained
at www.ICGtesting.com
Printed in the USA
LVOW03s0706090617

537529LV00002B/19/P